Flea Market GARDEN STYLE

CAROLINE McKENZIE

Flea Market GARDEN STYLE

168

54

122

140

CONTENTS

CHAPTER ONE

FIND YOUR FLAIR

10 STYLE GUIDE
Get inspired and discover your favorite looks with these decorative garden ideas.

24 A NEW DEAL
Vintage accessories from ladders to mirrors give your space plenty of style.

30 IN WITH THE OLD
Think beyond store-bought planters with these soulful touches of decor.

38 BENCH PRESS
These potting benches will inspire you to toil your soil in style.

42 HIGH-FLYING REAL ESTATE
Birdhouses add interest to your yard while attracting some feathered friends.

48 TALL ORDERS
Take your garden to new heights with clever vertical installations.

54 SMALL WONDERS
Get away from it all and find your happy place with creative "she shed" ideas.

64 CHARM TO TABLE
Discover some picture-perfect alfresco dining spaces for your next meal.

70 LIGHT THE WAY
Keep the garden joy going after sunset with a variety of dreamy illuminations.

76 MINIATURE GARDENS
Bigger is not always better, as these adorable installations can attest.

CHAPTER TWO

GET INSPIRED

82 OVER THE RAINBOW
Lush florals add a big dose of personality to this tiny California garden.

90 WORLDS AWAY
A compact urban backyard lives large thanks to a hip layout and decor.

96 FRONT & CENTER
A lush lawn shows a backyard isn't the only place to have a glorious garden.

106 BLUE STREAK
Pops of royal blue add vivacious charm to a magical garden in Quebec City.

116 ZEN & NOW
A former rock garden gets a flowery makeover with plenty of curb appeal.

122 SECRET SPACES
A rehabilitation expert transforms his own space into an ingenious retreat.

132 COUNTRY STRONG
A flower farm is home base for a family cabin that's bursting with charm.

CHAPTER THREE

DIY GARDEN PROJECTS

140 LIGHT UP YOUR YARD

142 IT'S SO TWEET!

144 CHECKED OUT

146 WINGING WAYS

148 LAND A FISH

150 BUZZWORTHY FUN

152 FRAME IT

154 MEDICINAL MAGIC

156 PEEK-A-BOO

158 WHEEL DEAL

160 FIRE IN THE HOLE

162 STYLISH STORAGE

164 SPREAD CHEER

166 FOR THE BIRDS

168 SIMPLE GARDEN GLOWS

170 POINT THE WAY TO THE PARTY

172 KEEPING WATCH

174 CRATE EXPECTATIONS

176 BRIGHT, BIG & BEAUTIFUL

178 TROPICAL DREAM

180 GARDEN CANDY

182 10 MORE EASY IDEAS

Anything goes when it comes to forging your own flea market style in your outdoor space. The key is to have some fun!

Turn your outdoor space into a retreat you'll love with fresh takes on favorite flea market finds.

Welcome to *Flea Market Garden Style*, where we are well rooted in a decidedly unstuffy approach to landscapes. We're firm believers that gardens look best when they are lush and layered—if (ahem) just a smidge unkempt. As far as we're concerned, the more varied and abundant the flora, the better!

We also have a soft spot for outdoor spaces brimming with old pieces—from cast-off kettles to architectural elements—that have been given new life. Whether you gravitate toward romantic or rustic looks or if you prefer a modern edge, we're all about growing your own totally unique style.

This book celebrates the best of the perfectly imperfect aesthetic with hundreds of fresh ideas for planters, lighting, furniture and more. You'll find inspiration on how to repurpose quirky items such as teacups and window panes into outdoor delights, plus tons of other tips and tricks to help transform your space with flea market finds and salvaged junk. And you'll get inspired by many gorgeous gardens, large and small. Plus, discover more than two dozen easy, fun and budget-friendly DIY projects to put into action. Get ready to chart your own course down the garden path.

—*Caroline McKenzie*

APPUCCINO
SOUP

CHAPTER ONE

FIND YOUR FLAIR

Find Your Flair

STYLE GUIDE

There's only one rule when it comes to nailing down a flea market inspired look—embrace what you love. Here, ideas for charting your own course.

OUT OF AFRICA

Bring a little of the African continent into your backyard with these colorful designs.

WHAT TO LOOK FOR

* mosaics * cobalt, umber and other strong colors * pools of water * pierced-metal lanterns * palms

1

1 **COURTYARD COLORS** Blue-and-white tiles on a patio's steps match a decorative bistro set. Containers with a citrus tree, papyrus and fragrant lavender add atmosphere. 2 **CHIC SHADE** Retreat from the sun with an open-sided canvas tent that mimics a poolside pavilion. 3 **NIGHTTIME AMBIENCE** Getting the lighting right for a perfect evening on the patio is essential. Look for inexpensive pierced-metal Moroccan-style lanterns to hold candles. 4 **COOL PERFECTION** Little water features, such as this delightful pond with a tile border, are the perfect contrast to the bright-green pickerelweed.

Plants, plates and vintage finds can be combined to achieve the desired look.

1 **PLATE PASSION** Collect an armful of mismatched plates from a junk store and attach them to a fence painted in romantic pink and white. Finish the look with a jug of cut flowers positioned on a table. 2 **SCENTS AND SENSIBILITY** Old metal buckets and scrolled metal furniture are perfect for the romantic style. Choose scented plants, such as lavender, rosemary and thyme. 3 **REGENCY DRAMA** You could just imagine sipping tea from bone china cups. Surround your bistro set with climbing roses on a pergola, arch or other support. 4 **THE STAGE IS SET** Use cushions, pastel colors and distressed objects to get the look.

Lovely
Vintage
ROMANTIC VINTAGE
Transform part of your yard into your favorite spot by lavishing it with truly feminine details.
WHAT TO LOOK FOR
* cushions * scented flowers and herbs * scrolled metal furniture * pastels * decorative objects
Hit the flea markets and garage sales, mix old with new, and use pink and white for a scene out of a Jane Austen novel.
4

MODERN MAGIC

Clean lines and understated colors keep the emphasis on the glory of the grounds.

WHAT TO LOOK FOR

* corrugated or sheet metal to create furniture or privacy screens
* succulents or other monochromatic plants
* simple furniture that's functional
* wooden decks

ENGLISH ELEGANCE

Meandering florals and traditional furnishings are favorites for a reason—they never go out of fashion!

WHAT TO LOOK FOR

* scrolling metals and white trellises * peonies, climbing roses, snapdragons and other time-honored favorites * brass or metal lampposts * low side tables

COASTAL CALM

Whether or not you live near water, you can still create seaside charm with inventive touches.

WHAT TO LOOK FOR

* pebbles * rope * lobster pots * driftwood * seashells * buoys or floats * calm coastal colors

Clever planting among your seafaring curiosities can make them look as if they've been there for decades.

1

1 **THE CRUNCH OF STONES** Pebbles used on your pathways give the feel that you are carefully making your way down to the beach. Old lobster pots and aged, weathered wooden boxes, chairs and floats here and there add to the seaside feel. 2 **ROPED IN** Grab a length of rope and coil it to form the base for other objects, such as old cork floats used as planters for small succulents. Seashells and a wooden bird heighten the effect. 3 **MOBILE CORNER** Use a shop-bought seaside mobile and suspend it in a corner of your yard (or make your own). 4 **MAKE WAVES** Give your fence a beachy feel by styling the top into a wavy line and painting it a light blue-green.

A TOUCH OF WHIMSY

Anything-goes colors and sweet antiques up the charm factor in gardens that are overflowing with plants and personality.

WHAT TO LOOK FOR
* unexpected elements such as worn chairs and household objects * perennials in varied and contrasting hues * curving trellises with climbers

ECLECTIC EDGE

Candy-colored kitsch and overgrown grounds make an unexpected but eye-pleasing pair.

WHAT TO LOOK FOR
* varied decor (such as this striped chair and bold pop art pieces) * an abundance of plants, no matter the type, size or color

Search for tools, blunt saws or wheels that are well past their prime to enhance your yard.

1 **SEAL THE DEAL** Old pipes of different widths have been cut and sealed at the base to hold small pools of water. To achieve the look, partially fill them with cement. 2 **WAREHOUSE CASTOFFS** Train your eye to hunt for industrial finds such as these old metal boxes—they make great planters for a group of succulents and can be artfully arranged. 3 **IN THE ROUND** An old rusty wheel doubles as a container for a variety of succulents—and nestled in the background is a discarded tool to carry on the theme. 4 **PIPE DREAM** We thought we'd show you this awesome pipe divider—it's both sculptural and spectacular—to stoke your enthusiasm for all things metal!

INDUSTRIAL CHIC

Industrial metal pieces left outdoors make fantastic decorations or cool containers for plants.

WHAT TO LOOK FOR

* aged tin cans * rusty tools * cogs, wheels and bits of machinery * contrasting bright-green foliage

Look for industrial pipes of different lengths and use them to create an attractive partition.

4

MORE IS MORE

Whatever your taste, there are simple ways to achieve incredible looks in your own yard, with the right flea market, thrift shop or yard sale treasures.

WHAT TO LOOK FOR

* old tools * metal watering cans * colorful fabrics or painted furniture * wooden crates and pallets * anything that catches your eye!

Like your garden itself, it pays to let your yard develop over time, adding new elements as you see fit.

1

To get the jungle look, you need plants that are big and bold—and, preferably, fast growing.

1 **HOMESTEAD HANGOUT** Search for old tools, vintage watering cans and buckets to adorn this productive area of the yard.
2 **COLORFUL KITSCH** Hunt for decor items in vibrant patterns and textures, or repaint items to introduce more color.
3 **JUNGLE FEELING** Re-create the tropics with exotic large-leaf plants and enhance the look with flea market finds, such as vintage signs, hanging lanterns and bistro sets. 4 **FARM FRIENDLY** Untreated woods, repurposed shipping pallets, burlap accents and galvanized buckets add to a homespun vibe. 5 **ON DISPLAY** This barn is cleverly used as a backdrop for a collection of flea market objects.

Find Your Flair

A NEW DEAL

Vintage accessories can go a long way toward helping you put together a garden you'll love for years.

STEP IT UP

Consider displaying your plants on raised platforms—or use old ladders from the flea market as climbing frames for rambling plants.

1

1 **DISCARDED CHARM** Rambling roses embrace an old discarded ladder propped against the back of a barn. 2 **VEGGIE GOOD** Temporarily store your vegetables as an attractive display in a sheltered spot. An old tub lends charm; a pair of pots hold lettuce and chicory. 3 **PAIRED UP** Group plants, such as (from top) bellflower, lobelia, silverbush and coleus, in pairs on a stepladder for dramatic effect. 4 **HIGH-RISE BLOOMS** An old ladder, secured against a tree, is the perfect place to hang cut flowers from the yard in galvanized watering cans. 5 **CLIMBING TO GLORY** Don't own an aged ladder? Get one from a flea market or junk shop.

1 **SHADY SECRET** A decorative window frame gets the mirror treatment and sheds light in a shady section, hinting at a secret room beyond. 2 **MIRROR IMAGE** Position a small mirror on a fence in a semishaded area to bring in more light. 3 **GO TO PIECES** This beautiful mosaic water feature adds vibrant color—and the mirrors suggest that the area is much bigger. 4 **MEDIEVAL LOOK** Find an unusual frame, such as this stone-look piece, put a mirror on the back and then place it on a plain wall to add interest. 5 **DOUBLE TAKE** What looks like a window into another part of the yard is an arch-shaped mirror placed on a wall and surrounded by a trellis.

MIRROR MIRROR

Who's the fairest of them all? Mirrors have an undeniable ability to add depth to a garden or hinting there is another "room"—even though one doesn't exist at all!

To trick the eye, be sure that your image is not obvious when you first approach the mirror: Angle it slightly away from you.

TOUCH OF GLASS

Flowers are glorious, but they are short-lived. There's no such "pane" with glass! Use the right type in the right location, and you'll have color throughout the year.

For a vibrant display, choose colored glass. Thrift- and junk-store finds provide years of pleasure on a budget.

1

1 **WINDOW DRESSING** A glass partition adds a splash of classic charm to this veranda. 2 **WALL ART** Gather some colored bottles and stack them in a tall gap to enhance a wall, then sit back and watch the light dance off them. 3 **PERGOLA PRIDE** Attach some colored glass panes to the back of a pergola; they'll make a neat screen—and let the light shine through. 4 **BOTTLE BRILLIANCE** Collect colored bottles and use them to create a backdrop, adding quirky dimension to your yard. 5 **LIGHT KNOW-HOW** Figure out the direction in which your garden faces and use that to set up your glass piece where the sun will best show it off.

Find Your Flair

IN WITH THE OLD

Think beyond store-bought planters and fill your garden with soulful, unexpected decor.

For displays blooming with sentimental value, look for crates bearing the names of favorite places.

1

1 **PACK IT UP** Old shipping containers were built to take a beating, making them ideal for surviving the elements. 2 **POUR IT ON** Turn a kitchen basic into a decorative garden element by placing blooms directly in it. 3 **HANGING OUT** This "chandelier" features a cast-iron wagon wheel with terra-cotta pots suspended from jute twine. 4 **BACKYARD DISPLAY** Whether hung upright or on their sides, wooden storage bins are a durable way to corral plants and party essentials alike. 5 **TO THE LETTER** Tuck succulents inside metal lettering, salvaged from old signage, for bright pops of color and to-the-letter style.

> There are no limits on what you can repurpose for garden delights—let your imagination run wild!

1 **RECYCLED CHARM** Old tin cans make a no-fuss vessel for simple arrangements. 2 **LOOKING BACK** Reflect natural light and extend the view by placing a vintage mirror among your plantings. 3 **KETTLE'S ON** Add whimsy with an antique teapot. (Teacups and coffee kettles will pour on the same appeal.) If planting items directly in the crockery, line with gravel to ensure proper drainage. 4 **TAKE A SEAT** Old chairs lend a sculptural but homey element, with a worn-out seat just the spot to nestle blossoms. 5 **UNEXPECTED DELIGHT** Replace existing light bulb sockets with plastic pots—painted the same shade as the chandelier—to create a verdant display overhead.

An indigo paint job gives the fixture a fresh new finish that stands out against the backdrop of greenery.

5

TIME FOR TEA

Unloved and unwanted, these beautiful thrift store china cups and saucers work perfectly as plant pots. You don't need to drill any holes in the bottom, but make sure you water the plants sparingly.

SUPER SUCCULENT A two-handled cup is suspended from a hook with colorful cord. OPPOSITE PICTURE PERFECT This little alpine planting contrasts beautifully with a petite bright-blue cup and saucer, proving even small details make a big impact.

1 **GET THE LOOK** Coral bead looks stunning with this matching cup and saucer. 2 **SMALL BUT SWEET** China cups are the perfect size to hold scented roses. 3 **DAINTY DELIGHT** Cushion pink flowers on a bed of green leaves in an eye-catching enamel teapot. 4 **DUSKY DAYLIGHT** Bone china cups make great tea-light holders—you can see the glow through the sides of the cup.

Dainty china
takes on new life
as part of a garden
theme—with plenty
of affordable options
for sale at local
flea markets!
4

Find Your Flair

BENCH PRESS

Gardens require tending! Let these potting benches inspire you to toil your soil in style.

NEUTRAL TERRITORY

Decorative accents, such as bunting and baskets, in cool tones of gray make for a calm aesthetic. The zinc-topped bench provides a very durable surface that will acquire a striking patina over time.

HEARTFELT

Folksy artwork and tchotchkes, plus a quirky bright-pink planter crafted from felt, give this ramshackle work area style in (garden) spades.

MOD SQUAD

Clean lines and a graphic black-and-white color palette lend a hip vibe to this homemade bench and privacy screen. Pops of pink and orange enhance the look.

COLOR CRUSH

An ordered-from-a-catalog potting bench is taken up a notch, thanks to a vibrant coat of coral paint. (Keeping the top white adds cottage-y contrast.)

TAKING A STAND

An old nightstand provides a coveted workspace in a compact garden. The pull-out drawer, complete with its original hardware, protects tools from the elements.

SPLENDOR IN THE GRASS

The beauty of this in-the-field bench? The simple raw-wood piece doesn't detract from the surrounding scenery. Bonus: It's light enough to move as needed.

MIX IT UP

A hutch? Open shelving? Pull-out drawer? This petite workspace packs it all in. Plus, the wood tones smartly match the brick for a cohesive look.

SEW SMART

An antique sewing table, outfitted with a plywood top, provides a work surface blanketed with storied style. The slats above make use of the paneled exterior wall.

WELL-GROUNDED

Yes, work surface is important, but so is the storage. This greenhouse spot leaves plenty of room for stashing large items such as food crates and bushel baskets.

SCREEN TIME

This no-fuss wood bench gets the job done without detracting from the ornate garden shed it abuts. The bottom cabinet was smartly designed with a lock and protective screen to keep curious critters out.

A bench placed beneath an overhang provides welcome shade for newly potted plants.

Find Your Flair

HIGH-FLYING REAL ESTATE

From palatial to simple but pretty, birdhouses can add interest to your yard while attracting some winged friends.

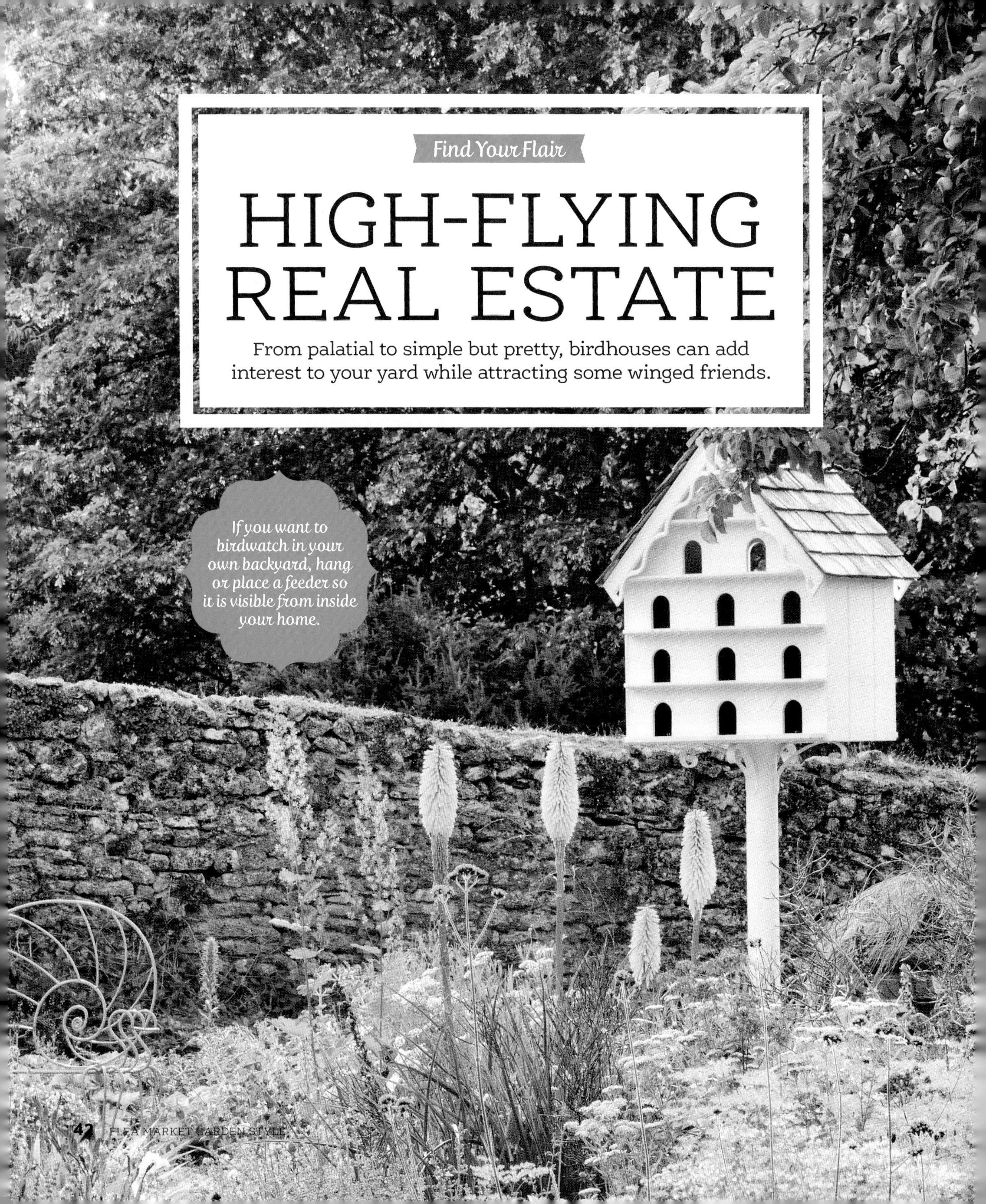

If you want to birdwatch in your own backyard, hang or place a feeder so it is visible from inside your home.

RUSTIC CHARM This birdhouse has been created from old bits of wood. You can find some in a junkyard or repurpose an old fence.
OPPOSITE FOCAL POINT Position a dovecote at the end of the yard to draw the eye and attract flighty friends.

TERRACED HOUSES These graduated boxes make a colorful feature and provide perches for the birds. OPPOSITE **LOVE A DOVE** A colorful birdhouse contrasts beautifully with the plumage of these birds and the lush greenery of a backyard.

In cold weather,
birdhouses provide
a safe place for
these animals
to snuggle up
and get warm.

1 **STAND ALONE** Birdhouses can be attached to anything: trees, walls or on their own poles. 2 **GRAY GARDEN** Here's something to inspire: a magnificent bird home made of sculpted cement! 3 **ELABORATE LIVING** Bird abodes can be simple or much more complex. This is a cottage-style house, complete with a faux chimney. 4 **TEAPOT TREAT** A colorful teapot makes a perfect home for a small bird. You can create a wooden lid that includes a perch and entranceway. 5 **THROUGH THE ROOF** You can attract different winged creatures (like bees and butterflies) by converting birdhouses into colorful planters.

5

Find Your Flair

TALL ORDERS

Take your garden to new heights with easy installations that aptly utilize vertical spaces.

BARNWOOD STORAGE

A motley crew of weathered boards was pieced together to create a rustic, no-frills spot for displaying succulents and other potted plants.

STICK DISPLAY

Lengths of hazel branches, lashed together with rope, offer a textured, sturdy design from which you can suspend wire baskets planted with colorful annuals.

TIN CAN GARDEN

Old coffee tins (washed clean of grounds) are strung from colorful yarn and planted with organic lettuce to create a kitchen garden within a compact space.

PALLET CONSOLE

White spray paint gives this shipping pallet a cottage vibe. Two-by-fours adhere to horizontal joints, creating shelves for displaying potted herbs and storing tools.

PAINTED TRELLIS

Purchased at a hardware store, a raw-wood garden trellis becomes a vibrant focal point thanks to a hot-pink paint job. Yellow climbing roses complete the look.

LADDER LEDGE

A simple wooden ladder provides a multitiered surface for showcasing flora of all types. The cascading greenery adds movement to the verdant vignette.

RECYCLED TIMBER SHELVES

Dozens of succulents planted in matching terra-cotta pots help to balance out the "ceiling" of this eclectic patio garden with the layered scene below.

MATTRESS SPRINGS DECOR

This unexpected garden element is suspended from a simple wooden frame with a window box planter below; the vines grow along the old bedsprings.

FLORAL BUNTING

Bundles of lavender and other herbs hang from a birch log, adding a bunting-like element to an exterior wall and allowing garden clippings to dry in the sun.

HERB GRID

Simple strips of lattice, adhered in a windowpane-esque arrangement, creates a grid for hanging tin cans that are planted with a variety of herbs.

Just as they coexist in nature, vivid blues and greens make happy companions in garden decor.

SQUARE AWAY

This vertical screen, made with rusty industrial frames, helps divide the garden. It is planted with varieties chosen specifically for their interesting foliage and textures, which are fully appreciated up close.

A living wall is a beautiful solution for creating privacy or obstructing an unsightly view, like an AC unit.

IN THE POCKET

Store-bought planting pockets, filled with a variety of herbs and flowers, add a splash of color to a dull fence or wall—and can be easily moved.

PRETTY AS A PICTURE

A homemade wooden frame is a novel way to create a living display of drought-tolerant succulents such as hens and chicks.

CLIMBING UP

Steel wires are used to create a framework on which climbers can grow. This example features a deep-purple clematis against a bold orange wall.

CAN DO

Metal cans suspended from threaded and knotted rope create a unique, rustic wall planter. Here, they're planted with *Erigeron strigosus* (daisy fleabane).

Find Your Flair

SMALL WONDERS

These varied "she sheds" let you get away from it all—right in your own backyard.

THE TEAROOM

You'd probably never guess this frilly retreat was once a run-of-the-mill shed purchased unfinished at a big-box hardware store. Now swathed in pastel colors and charming floral prints, it offers up an unapologetically feminine space to sip tea and snack on treats that are as sweet as the surroundings.

THE CRAFT STUDIO

Gingerbread trim, soothing blue-green paint and a smart antique clock make this formerly boring brick structure feel downright magical. Inside, a large crafting table and ample storage for supplies create a space where your imagination can run just as wild.

THE OUTDOOR OFFICE

Have work to do? Finish it in a space that feels worlds away from the chaos of a traditional office. This shed is especially bright and airy with the addition of antique French doors at the entrance. Pale-blue paint on the interior creates an equally serene effect.

Simple embellishments such as a wood remnant at the peak of the roof add heaps of charm.

THE OPEN-AIR ESCAPE

A sophisticated shade of barely there green gives this shed's simple design an elevated look. Work stations flank the left and right sides of the small space, while a bench in the back provides the ideal spot for curling up with a new book. (Twinkle lights let you enjoy the space after dark, too!)

Use potted plants to make a new structure feel nestled in, as though it's been there all along.

THE GARDEN FOLLY

Salvaged windows and a living roof planted with native grasses make this shed feel like something out of a fairy tale. In stark contrast to its exterior, the inside is thoroughly modern—just big enough to house a built-in bar, complete with a wine fridge and ice maker.

Black siding may be unusual, but it's reminiscent of tree bark when paired with a planted roof.

THE MOD ABODE

A shipping container gets a second act as an outdoor kitchen and dining space. The clean lines of this industrial piece are amped up with a knock-your-socks-off shade of tangerine. And the steel framework allows for the weight of dozens of potted plants on the roof.

THE COZY RETREAT

Achieve a homey style effortlessly. Add hanging textiles, sheer drapes, knickknack-filled shelves, comfy seats, rugs and that blanket knitted by Grandma for a place you'll love no matter the season.

Create your own dream escape in the backyard. You deserve some "me time"!

THE SEWING ROOM

If you don't have space for another outbuilding, convert part of your existing garden shed into a comfortable spot for sewing supplies and other projects.

THE COUNTRY HAVEN

Sink into a Lloyd Loom wicker chair as you write a letter at the pretty, lace-covered table. A charming lampshade completes the look.

Pick out calming colors or shades that say something about you and the way you want to live.

4 MORE WAYS TO DECORATE

1

2

3

4

1 **SHABBY CHIC** If your shed is big enough, move in a sofa and a wingback chair for added comfort as you go through your paperwork or carry out your creative projects. 2 **BRIGHTEN UP** Bold and beautiful fabrics such as these are serious eye-catchers that will lift your spirits on any dull, gray day. 3 **WOODEN WARMTH** Varnishing the floor of your shed will add warmth and complement the bright-white walls that serve as the backdrop for carefully chosen decorations. 4 **LIGHT AND EASY** Accents in soft hues elevate any space. Pick pastel blues for your paint and textiles and choose decorations to support your color choices.

Find Your Flair

CHARM TO TABLE

Please be seated! These picture-perfect alfresco dining spaces are brimming with easy-to-replicate ideas.

A mix of seating options gives off a relaxed vibe that encourages guests to sit and stay awhile.

DOUBLE DUTY This cozy backyard maximizes space with dining tables placed in the atrium and on the adjoining patio. The all-white furnishings create a cohesive style between the two areas. OPPOSITE **QUILT TO LAST** Add homey charm to any outdoor tablescape by layering in an antique quilt in lieu of a standard tablecloth. The handsome stitching and faded fabrics will take the edge off even the newest outdoor dining table.

1 **UP AND AWAY** A simple iron table and chairs take on a sophisticated air when placed below a magical canopy of voluminous wisteria hanging from a pergola. 2 **SIGNATURE COLOR** From the silk tablecloth and calico bunting to the luscious peonies strung from the spindle-back chairs, shades of pink pull together this romantic tablescape. 3 **GLOBAL APPEAL** Colorful paper lanterns add warmth and fun when displayed over a simple backyard spread. 4 **LESS IS MORE** A teak table with clean lines complements, rather than competes with, the handsome olive trees surrounding the area. Chic accents such as the bronze lanterns and a patterned area rug elevate the look of the outdoor setting.

From a cup
of coffee to a
formal fete,
an alfresco meal
serves up time
to commune
with nature.
4

1

2

3

1 **FLY HIGH** Whimsical die-cut butterflies, scattered jewel "confetti" and personalized menus wrapped in bright tissue paper make a colorful display. The key to pulling off this bold look is starting with a solid-color tablecloth. 2 **NATURAL WONDER** To make this floral table runner, pick long grasses and wildflowers and weave them into garland the length of the table. Complement with matching napkins; tie a few blades of grass around each and tuck in a flower. 3 **AUTUMN HARVEST** This simple fall bounty table requires no florist skills, just a few sprigs picked from the garden and some windfall (or freshly picked) apples. 4 **SIMPLE CHARM** Fill old glass milk bottles or Mason jars with homegrown annual flowers to brighten up a table for a quick get-together. 5 **LIGHTEN UP** Small paper votive holders are lovely with sun shining through them during the day—and they're even more dramatic in the evening, filled with battery-operated flickering votive candles. 6 **SEASONAL SENSE** A crafty idea: Use a sharp knife and a spoon to hollow out mini gourds; arrange them on a strip of wood and pop in pillar candles for this autumnal centerpiece.

To make cut flowers last longer, trim an inch off the stems every few days. Cut at an angle so the stems "drink" more water.
4

5

6

Find Your Flair

LIGHT THE WAY

Keep the garden joy going after the sun sets with dreamy illuminations of all shapes, sizes and styles.

TWINKLE TIME An outdoor staple for a reason, dainty string lights cast a glow that's equal parts chic and whimsical. (Hang them vertically for an extra-enchanted look.) OPPOSITE RUSTIC APPEAL Elevate an outdoor table with an assortment of towering candleholders along with smaller candles. Unfinished wood will feel at home in a casual garden setting.

Outdoor candlelight casts a flattering glow that beckons guests to linger.

1 **GLASS HALF FULL** For a can-do look, skip a fussy chandelier; place sand in the bottoms of Mason jars, then add tea lights or battery-operated fairy lights and suspend them on overhead limbs. 2 **PETAL PUSHER** Dot your garden with pressed-flower candles. The earthy look will cast an organic glow that feels at home amid the flora and fauna. 3 **TORCH GLOW** Add light and height with the addition of rattan garden torches. Whether you tuck them among hedges or arrange them in a uniform line, they'll bring a fiery element to your yard. 4 **UNDERSTATED AURA** Take simple tea lights up a notch with ornate glass votives. Display them in grouped vignettes to amplify the light, and add height with delicate floral lights like those shown here.

4

1 **BUDGET FRIENDLY** This funky space is created with a tablecloth used as a canopy, paper lanterns suspended with fishing wire and napkins attached to strings with clothespins. 2 **WATER WONDERS** Add floating candles and flowers picked from the garden to a small water feature on a patio. 3 **DOWN BELOW** For a truly high-tech look to your contemporary garden, install LED lighting around the underside of tables and benches. This table doubles as a propane firepit for added glow. 4 **HIGH LIGHTS** Integrating lighting into your garden can add an extra dimension—and a higher level of security, too. These uplighters show off the row of trees.

4

Find Your Flair

MINIATURE GARDENS

Who says bigger is better? These teeny-tiny gardens have a magical, mystical appeal and are so fun to create.

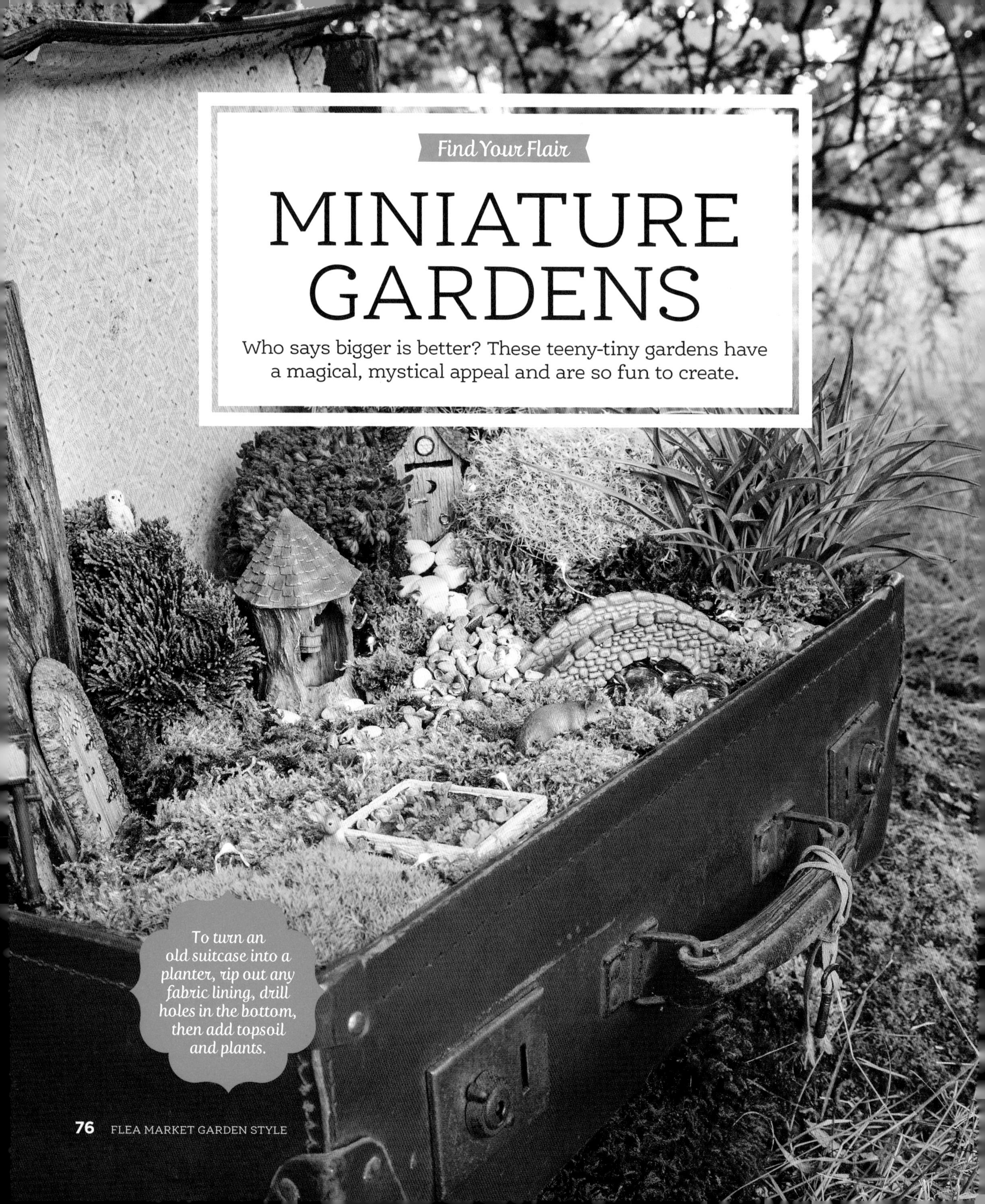

To turn an old suitcase into a planter, rip out any fabric lining, drill holes in the bottom, then add topsoil and plants.

RIGHT TO SCALE Mixed alpine plants create a miniature garden in a salt-glazed container. Gravel and beach stones act as mulch to help the soil retain moisture. OPPOSITE **STORY-WORTHY** A vintage suitcase is the container for this tiny garden. Store-bought ornaments are used to set up a woodland scene. There are no flowers in this garden so the ornaments can take center stage among miniature evergreen trees, moss and alpines.

PLAY TIME An old square terra-cotta planter was used to create this miniature garden with a picket fence made from clothespins, a lawn composed of grass clippings and stepping stones made from flat rocks. OPPOSITE **TELLING TALES** A compact fairy garden—on wheels—is a fun and quirky project to complete with the kids and a great way to reuse an old wheelbarrow that is past its prime.

CAUTION
FAIRIES LIVE
HERE

CHAPTER TWO

GET INSPIRED

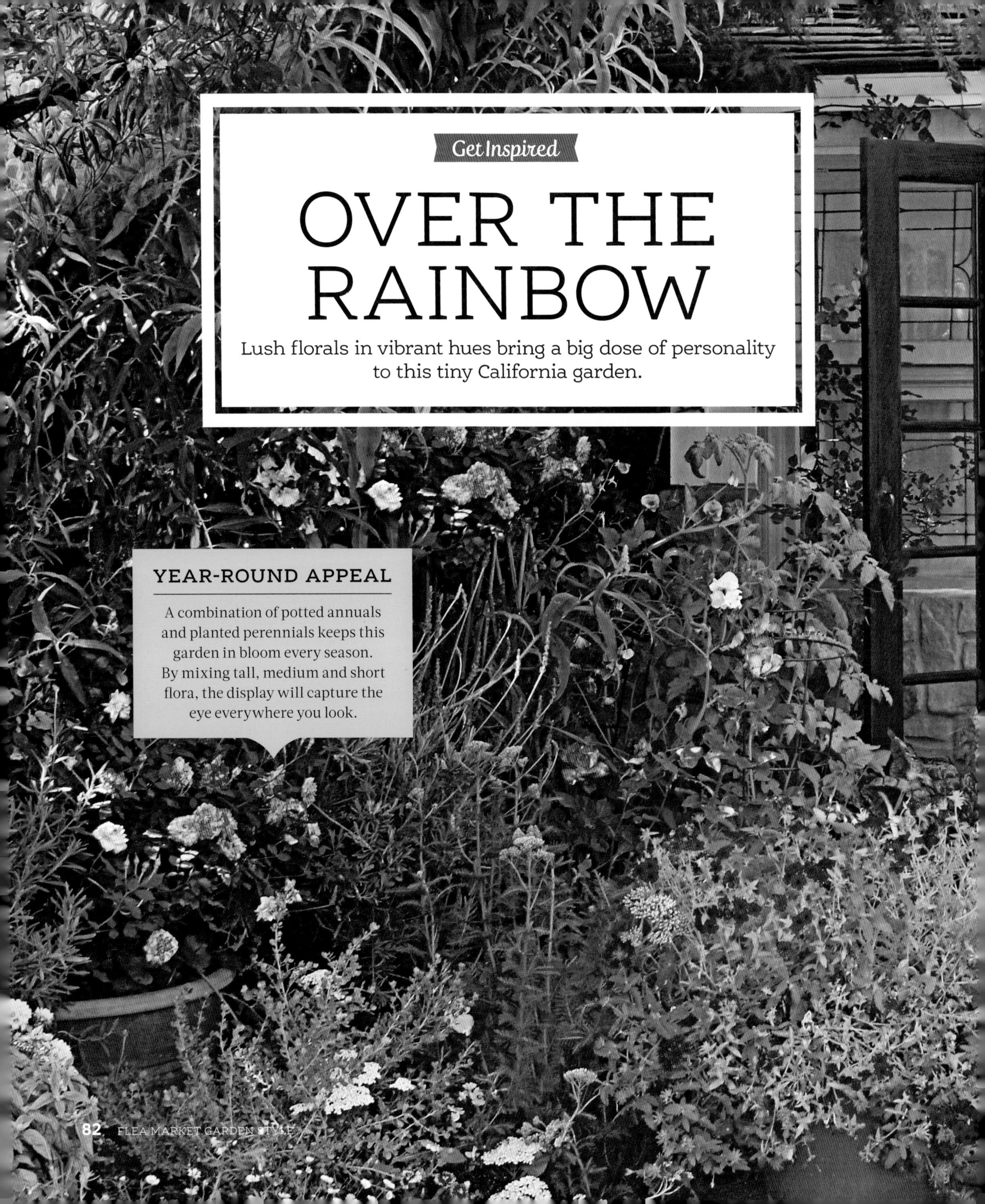

Get Inspired

OVER THE RAINBOW

Lush florals in vibrant hues bring a big dose of personality to this tiny California garden.

YEAR-ROUND APPEAL

A combination of potted annuals and planted perennials keeps this garden in bloom every season. By mixing tall, medium and short flora, the display will capture the eye everywhere you look.

Junkyard doors and windows were used to construct this petite "teahouse."

It started with a rosebush. Or, to be more specific, 12 rosebushes. "I'd never had the slightest interest in gardening," says Californian Patty Fernandez, who will never forget the moment that all changed. "I was in my car, driving by a nursery and they had all these roses in bloom. I made a hard left and went straight for them." Although she'd never planted a thing before, she left with a dozen billowing rosebushes and a single gardening book. Much to her surprise, she had great success with her roses. "They lived. They grew. They flourished. The entire thing astounded and captivated me," she recalls.

As the roses blossomed, Fernandez began to connect her newfound passion of gardening with two other hobbies: art and travel. "I've always loved Claude Monet's work and have visited his home in Giverny, France, numerous times," explains Fernandez, who became particularly enthralled with the famed artist's garden after she took up the pastime herself. While she readily admits she is "no Monet," her inspiration for a backyard filled with color and softness came from the artist's carefree but peaceful garden.

It took the better part of two decades to transform those rosebushes and an otherwise unremarkable yard into that pastoral reality. But Fernandez and her budding green thumb kept at it and eventually the blank canvas was blanketed in soft, sweet flowers such as climbing roses, snapdragons and creeping phlox. "Not everything has worked exactly as I originally intended it to. But I slowly but surely began figuring out what would thrive where and when," she says.

Over the years, Fernandez also started acquiring wonderfully weathered accessories and furnishings that add to the grounds' French country flair. Lacy parasols, petite bistro chairs and wrought-iron daybeds all come together to give the garden a certain je ne sais quoi. "I love the way the decor reads as a natural extension of the landscaping," she says.

Fernandez says the yard has become a sanctuary of sorts for her. She spends as much time as possible tending to and enjoying her labor of love. "I live in a very regular house on a very regular street," she points out. "But there is nothing regular about my backyard. It's like stepping into another time and place." Turns out that impulse decision to stop at the nursery all those years ago was nothing short of a stroke of genius. Monet surely would approve.

COLLECT CALL Fernandez's extensive collection of vintage textiles includes dozens of floral tablecloths, which she rotates on outdoor tables throughout the year. OPPOSITE **GATE-KEEPER** The weathered wooden gate and fencing make a rustic foil to the frilly flowers.

No sweeping allowed! Windblown petals and branches create garden vignettes with unkempt whimsy.

"Lace tablecloths, vintage quilts—I believe in using pretty 'indoor' items outside, too," says Patty Fernandez.

AMAZING LACE

A broken patio umbrella becomes a garden's ethereal focal point when draped with vintage lace and suspended from a towering tree limb.

Curtain panels in outdoor fabrics like this black-and-white stripe give impact to low-key doorways.

1 **PAVE THE WAY** Simple stone pavers have a storybook feel thanks to the flowers bursting out between them. 2 **STRENGTH IN NUMBERS** This easily overlooked corner boasts more than a dozen types of flowers and plants that embody homeowner Fernandez's more-is-more mantra. 3 **SECOND ACT** The striking fountain was purchased at a local bed-and-breakfast's going-out-of-business sale. 4 **BED OF ROSES** Fernandez had to twist the arm of local antiques dealers to convince them to sell her the French iron daybed, which fits underneath the eaves of her shed lean-to.

A paper parasol adds a très chic element to a simple shed lean-to.

Get Inspired

WORLDS AWAY

This compact urban backyard lives large, thanks to hip accents and an even hipper layout.

FAIR-WEATHER FIND

Homeowner Laura Davis found a wooden table on eBay for less than $100. She removed dated paint, then scrubbed bleach into the top and left it in the sun to acquire a whitewashed look.

Look to native wildflowers to create an unfussy flower bed that's also incredibly low maintenance.

1 **READY TO ENTERTAIN** Laura Davis sets the table before a garden fete. Since she transformed her yard, it has become the site of many celebrations. 2 **BRIGHT IDEA** An electrician installed power sockets in the garden house to not only allow for task lamps, but also so Davis could string bistro lights along the courtyard, lending a romantic ambience after dark. 3 **SWING TIME** If this macramé swinging chair recalls a groovier time, it should! Davis found the hip relic on eBay for a steal and immediately knew it would be perfect for the garden house. The woven frame makes it easy to clean—a necessity, as it is exposed to the elements. 4 **MATERIAL WORLD** Textiles such as the ikat pillows and a woven pouf were integral in achieving a bohemian look. The textured elements bring warmth and softness.

It took a few years, but Laura Davis and her partner, Chris, inexplicably found their small urban backyard overrun. No, not with weeds or unwelcome critters, which you might expect. Instead, it was populated with something equally unsightly: sheds. Three of them in total, mismatched and all utter eyesores. "There was one when we bought the house, then we added one to store seasonal items, and finally we installed a third to serve as a workshop," recalls Davis. "They all seemed like good ideas at the time, but one day we realized we were rarely using them and missed having a backyard to enjoy and entertain in."

Ready to shed their sheds, they undertook a major clear out, culling down all the items into a few necessities that would fit into a utility closet. They then set about designing a year-round garden that maximized the small footprint and embodied their boho meets sophisticated style. "In such a small plot, it was important to make the layout work visually," Davis explains. "We settled on quite a formal-looking design with a garden house at the back and symmetrical raised beds to frame a new dining area—something I'd been dreaming about for years."

The first order of business was a concrete base for the garden house, as well as new fencing. While very practical, the latter proved to be Davis' first big, bold design decision: She chose horizontal planks painted an inky blue-green for a graphic and modern border. Next came the raised beds, which were built from run-of-the-mill cinder blocks but painted a crisp white that belies the humble materials. (The couple cut costs with

the bed materials so they could splurge on limestone pavers for the patio nestled between the beds.) Chris' company Distinguished Gardens oversaw the planting of the long, narrow beds, which were lined with pea gravel for drainage and then filled with compost and leaf mulch. "Chris is passionate about native plants and color, so he carefully planted our little beds with a select assortment of annuals and perennials so we have color throughout the season," Davis says.

Last but not least came the final "big job"—constructing and furnishing the new garden house. Davis decided to take her time with this task, furnishing it gradually using treasures from the likes of eBay and garage sales. "I become charmed by the thrill of the hunt, creating a bohemian style one piece at a time," she reveals. "I can't see myself getting bored of the style because I've learned anything natural and earthy looks timeless with a collected look." Something else she learned? Accent walls aren't just for inside the house. "I made the bold decision to paint one of the garden shed walls a high-impact black. Together with the white painted floors, it creates a polished, looks-good-enough-to-be-in-a-living-room look." Other niceties worthy of a living room include the antique writing desk, cushy textiles and alluring artwork.

Today, the urban oasis feels far away from the surrounding city bustle *and* the overcrowded space it once was. "We've enjoyed so many celebrations with friends and family in our finished garden. It's also become a fantastic space for me to work," explains Davis. "Gardens as small as this can be tricky, but ours proves they can live large with both style and function."

TRUNK INSPECTION Need storage? Try a handsome officer's trunk. (Savvy Davis scored it after it was discarded curbside.) This spacious piece conceals an assortment of garden tools and can also double as extra seating in a pinch. OPPOSITE **WORK IT** A firm believer in bringing the inside out, Davis placed an honest-to-goodness office desk in the summer house. Painted a few shades lighter than the interior walls, it lends a sophisticated element to the backyard retreat.

Simple task lighting makes the garden shed a functional space both day and night.

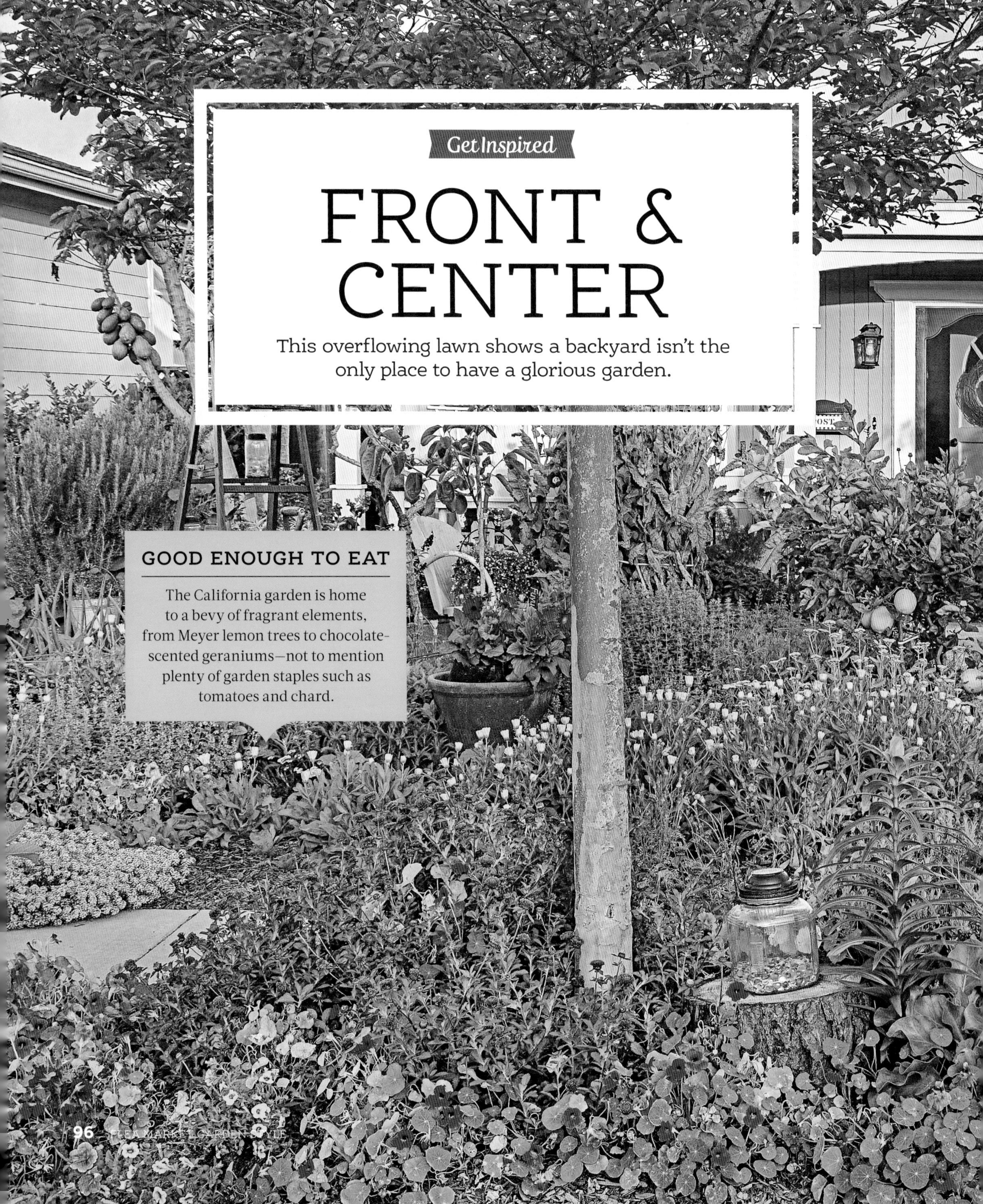

Get Inspired

FRONT & CENTER

This overflowing lawn shows a backyard isn't the only place to have a glorious garden.

GOOD ENOUGH TO EAT

The California garden is home to a bevy of fragrant elements, from Meyer lemon trees to chocolate-scented geraniums—not to mention plenty of garden staples such as tomatoes and chard.

1

1 **SEEING RED** The homeowner uses the same rusty-red paint to update various flea market finds she adds to the garden. Here, an old chair makes a handy perch for gardening necessities. 2 **FRUITY DELIGHTS** Cherries add delicious pops of color to the garden, which peaks in early June. 3 **LIGHT ON** Solar-powered lights, crafted by Henricks' daughter-in-law using antique glass jars and glass beads, are scattered throughout the garden for a fairylike feel at night. 4 **BUCKET LIST** Instead of investing in pricey planters, Henricks displays annuals in an ever-rotating assortment of galvanized buckets. Beyond-vibrant marigolds add to the colorful scene.

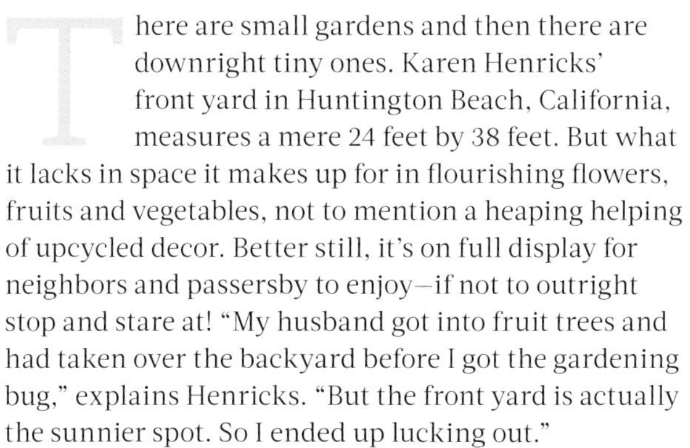

There are small gardens and then there are downright tiny ones. Karen Henricks' front yard in Huntington Beach, California, measures a mere 24 feet by 38 feet. But what it lacks in space it makes up for in flourishing flowers, fruits and vegetables, not to mention a heaping helping of upcycled decor. Better still, it's on full display for neighbors and passersby to enjoy—if not to outright stop and stare at! "My husband got into fruit trees and had taken over the backyard before I got the gardening bug," explains Henricks. "But the front yard is actually the sunnier spot. So I ended up lucking out."

The space wasn't without its challenges. Riddled with monkey grass, it took Henricks a "solid five years" to eradicate it completely. "I'd dig out a section and then sketch out what to plant in its place," she recalls.

Today, there's no monkey grass in sight, and the front yard is a mix of edible items (Swiss chard, papaya and squash, to name a few) along with beloved flowers (hollyhocks, poppies and geraniums are some of her favorites). "In a space this small, you really can't have 'sections'" she says. "You just plant where you can and see what takes off."

Nestled among the varied blossoms and vegetables are the aforementioned flea market finds. Henricks' favorite? One of her very first introductions to the garden—an old work ladder. "My husband brought it home and I thought, 'Hey! I'm going to paint that red and put it in the yard,'" she recalls. It's become a staple, if not symbol, of the bountiful display that, season after season and year after year, takes what a front yard can be to new heights.

"I want a garden that's full and easy to tend. That means changing course as nature sees fit," says Karen Henricks.

QUITE A HAUL

A wheelbarrow got a permanent parking spot in the garden. Here, it's planted with lobelia in a rainbow of hues. (Psst: It's lined with gravel to aid drainage.)

"Don't plan for whimsy! Just add objects as you find them and they speak to you," notes Henricks.

1 **ON THE FLY** Dainty flowers surround a dragonfly paver created from a craft-store mold. 2 **DIG IN** The old work ladder is held in place by befittingly scrappy means: It's tied with twine to a worn-out shovel inserted securely into the ground. 3 **LEMON AID** Dwarf Meyer lemons are ripe for the picking in the largely edible landscape. 4 **BORDER PATROL** The edge of the garden is lined with a tidy row of vibrant cosmos and nigellas.

Soften the base of a row of trees by planting vibrant annuals around each of the trunks.

4

Apple
Scented
Geranium
1

Enamelware is equally well suited for collecting garden goodies and for using as a colorful planter.

1 **FAUX REAL** An aluminum table and chairs are a dead ringer for an honest-to-goodness iron set. Henricks softened the look with a vintage floral tablecloth. 2 **STAKE OUT** Henricks crafts her own garden stakes, often pairing found twigs or branches with paint stirrers or wood scraps. She paints the latter her signature red, and then writes the plant name with a paint pen. 3 **CLEANUP ACT** In another installment of "my husband brought it home so I'm going to use it," she repurposed an old washing machine into a planter topped with a primitive birdhouse. It's a look that cleans up nicely. 4 **BERRY SPECIAL** Juicy, freshly picked blackberries are among the bounty found in the small front yard.

Get Inspired

BLUE STREAK

Striking pops of royal blue add vivacious charm to this verdant, completely magical Quebec City garden.

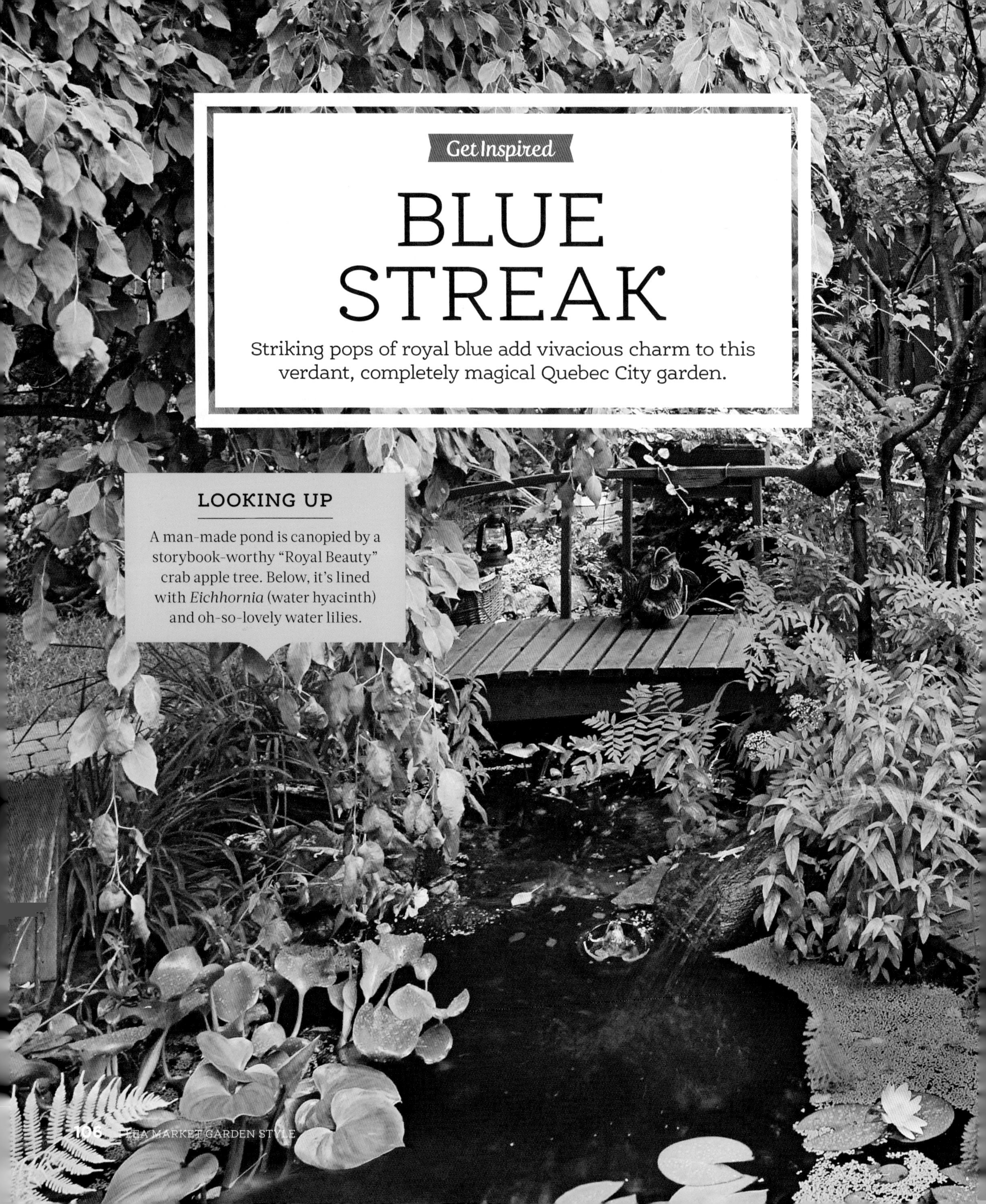

LOOKING UP

A man-made pond is canopied by a storybook-worthy "Royal Beauty" crab apple tree. Below, it's lined with *Eichhornia* (water hyacinth) and oh-so-lovely water lilies.

Decking placed at various heights allows you to create "rooms" within a single garden.

1 **ROCK AND ROLL** A past-its-prime rocking chair and wicker basket were revived with blue paint to become a fetching perch for purple petunias. 2 **LADY IN WAITING** Dubé transformed a folk art creation into a colorful garden display. 3 **GIVE THE GATE** White yarrow flowers and climbing *Vitis* spruce up a garden center gate and arbor. 4 **HANG LOOSE** Blue, red and orange flower pots (all painted by Dubé!) were strung along a chair to create a master of ceremonies for the character-filled garden.

Chrystiane Dubé and Roland Ratté do what they like. Case in point: After their children left for college, the Canadian couple made the bold decision to fill in the family swimming pool and create waves of a different sort. "Our house is in the center of Quebec City and not large by any means," Dubé explains. "The entire lot is 5,600 square feet and the backyard is just 40 by 60 feet. Getting rid of the swimming pool meant we could have more room for the garden of our dreams." What does a dream garden look like? For this couple, it was a shaded, layered space, brimming with upcycled and handmade treasures.

To put that dream into action they began by building a pond in the same spot where the pool had once been. ("The location was not lost on our kids," Dubé says. "They were initially underwhelmed by the replacement but finally came around.") The couple then installed paved trails fanning out from the new pond and around the front yard and backyard, which became the framework for a meandering garden design. They also built a small footbridge connecting two paths across the pond. "That was a deceptively simple project that added visual interest and a bit of storybook charm to the yard," Dubé says.

Though she had flowers on the brain, this gardener knew that trees needed to come first in their backyard overhaul. Although it's a relatively small garden, you'll find an abundance of trees, including a beguiling lilac tree dripping with blooms when in season and a now-mature "Royal Beauty" crab apple tree, which casts its magic over the pond, creating a shady border for foliage plants such as ostrich ferns. For the record, Dubé did get around to the flowers, adding an impressive array of perennials that dot the landscape, as well as annuals introduced each season to give the grounds additional color. ("I grow these under artificial light during the cold months," she says. "That's my winter hobby!")

3

4

Also in abundance: the color blue. What started as a bit of an homage to the old swimming pool soon became the garden's theme. "I just found myself very drawn to royal blue and it can now be seen everywhere. Over the years, we've even taken to calling the garden 'Mamie Blue.'" The striking shade not only wonderfully suits the verdant foliage found throughout the yard; it also makes a handsome hue for updating shabby garage-sale finds, which the pair soon found themselves constantly on the hunt for.

Indeed, over the years, the couple have become as enamored with whimsical garden decor as they are with the plants themselves. Today, playful ornaments—some found, some made—can be spotted at every turn. "Most of the furniture is handcrafted, then painted in blue. We really love thrift sales and delight in finding beautiful things at affordable prices that can be transformed with imagination and a little bit of blue paint," Dubé shares. "We do not throw anything away, we reuse and repurpose. We can find a use for everything!"

The result is undeniably charming. Interesting objects abound—from an old iron bed frame turned support for climbing plants, to a salvaged black streetlamp—in the welcoming garden.

The look isn't something only the homeowners relish; they've also found the local wildlife to be fans of the grounds. Countless varieties of birds, including blue jays, cardinals and turtle doves, have established homes in the trees and birdhouses the couple have crafted over the years. Families of squirrels, raccoons and skunks also visit, along with two ducks who come each spring to say "hello" before traveling to their final destination. "Keep in mind, we are in the city and this is all quite a feat," says Dubé, who wouldn't have it any other way. "We are very proud of our garden; it is beautiful in all seasons—whether under the snow or bursting with flowers. This is our little paradise, our Mamie Blue."

CHAIR-ISH THE MOMENT Chrystiane Dubé's first trek into the wild blue yonder was with these vintage wicker chairs, which she purchased for a mere $10 and overhauled with a quart of paint. OPPOSITE **STANDING TALL** A blue heron sculpture (carved from teakwood) stands proud amid a woolly border bed planted with ostrich ferns and an abundance of perennials.

Thoughtful additions such as antique streetlights and a freestanding stove add to the ambience.

BRIDGE THE GAP

A homemade footbridge, decorated with red pelargoniums, leads to the center of this quaint urban garden, where visitors can sit and relax in the peaceful surroundings.

"We tackle one new project a year. It's always such a joy to see them come to fruition in the spring," says homeowner Dubé.

SHOOTS AND LADDERS An old orchard ladder serves as a display for potted plants. OPPOSITE **TREE HOUSE** A beloved lilac tree brims with handmade birdhouses, making it even more of a crowd-pleaser.

Get Inspired

ZEN & NOW

A former rock garden now overflows with a bevy of flowers and come-as-you-are appeal.

Hang a mirror outdoors to help a dark or shaded spot feel brighter.

POP OUT

Add bursts of color to neutral decor, whether through pillows and blankets or vivid florals. An eclectic assortment of pots dress up the catalog sofa and chairs.

Maximize curb appeal with a front garden as lush and layered as one you'd typically find out back.

1

1 **PRIVACY ACT** A Manchurian pear tree adds a buffer to the close-to-the-road home. Out front, the old rock garden mixes with flowers such as zinnias and petunias. 2 **INTO THE BLUE** The homeowner treats herself to one new glazed pot each year. After nearly two decades, the collection is abundant. 3 **CONTAIN YOURSELF** A container garden thrills with calibrachoa and large, eye-catching canna lily.

Mothers pass on many things to their daughters. For Holly Fliniau, it's a love of gardening that has been handed down. "My mom loves plants, but lives at an extremely high elevation with fewer than 30 frost-free days a year," explains Fliniau, who had no sooner purchased a home in lower-elevation Denver than she found her mother planting perennials in her new yard. "Of course, she put it all in and then left so I had to learn to tend to it!"

Learn she did. Over the course of 20-plus years, she's taken what was once a rock garden in disrepair (a holdover from the previous owners) into something alive with flowers and thrifty treasures. Fliniau worked with her mother to measure where the sun hit and for how many hours per day, then sketched out a plan on notebook paper for a blueprint in the years to come. Along the way, the yard evolved into various rooms including a beer garden (where hops grow for brewing) and a sunroom that was once a garage. She also defined her garden style. "I'm all about wabi-sabi," says Fliniau. "It's a Japanese aesthetic that finds beauty and centering in things that are imperfect, impermanent and incomplete." With the garden ever-changing season to season and year to year, she has found her love for it a constant. (Charmed neighbors wander around as well, but she doesn't mind.) "This garden is my hobby. It's my joy." As always, a mother knows best.

ROOM WITH A VIEW To maximize outdoor living space, the garage was transformed into an open-air sunroom. Sophie the Bernese mountain dog approves. OPPOSITE **FITTING IN** The homeowner repainted the exterior—which was once a color bordering on neon green—a dark brown to create a more natural backdrop for the garden.

Don't neglect exterior walls! Consider them blank canvases to enliven your own unique style.

Get Inspired

SECRET SPACES

A rehabilitation expert faced a challenge when working on his multitiered yard before creating an ingenious retreat.

TRANQUIL FEEL The yard is sectioned off with a bamboo privacy screen, while a large umbrella shades an old table with contrasting vibrant-yellow chairs. OPPOSITE **DARK CORNER** To brighten up this shaded part of the yard, homeowner Steven Wells hung a skinny rectangular mirror framed with rustic wood.

1 **RUSTIC RETRO** These two cement pots are planted with succulents such as *Aloe juvenna* (tiger tooth aloe) and an echeveria. 2 **REST & RELAX** Wells uses his horticultural skills to help people get over spine and brain trauma, and designs gardens to help with rehabilitation. 3 **RED HOT** These cherry-colored pots provide a splash that fits seamlessly with the yard's overall theme. 4 **MODERN TAKE** This seating pod is a modern take on an arch or an arbor. Its striking hue stands out against a black-painted timber screen.

This calming backyard had a number of interesting attributes—it was on different levels, it sloped and was an odd shape—when Steven Wells first started working on it. But he knew right away that he wanted it to be a retreat, a place where he could display his eye for flea market-style objects.

It helped that his talents also lie in horticulture. He comes from a line of orchardists, seedsmen and market gardeners, and he had a wealth of gardening treasures he could use to enhance his yard.

Wells' aim was to create "destinations to stop and sit"—and he succeeded beyond his wildest dreams. His designs have provided seclusion and privacy and take full advantage of both sunny and shady spots in which he can sit back and relax.

It was his role in designing yards for people undergoing rehabilitation for spinal and head injuries that inspired Wells to lavish attention on his own yard: "In developing yards for others to enjoy for respite and relaxation, I understood the value of having my own space. It was important to have my yard, prioritize time to develop it and spend time working and relaxing in it."

Screening the garden has been of paramount importance to Wells, and he's never short of ideas. The screens are made of timber, some of which have been painted black, and are in varying heights to add interest. Elsewhere, climbing plants have been trained up the screens on a grid of wire as a living wall. Wells has carefully chosen species that grow well in the climate and soil.

The screens separate all levels of the garden and provide an element of surprise when you walk through it. By running screens with horizontal borders, he makes the yard also appear longer.

Wells introduced seating areas to take advantage of both the winter sun and the summer shade. Each has a splash of vibrant color as its focal point.

He calls the padded-bench seating area, built inside a wooden frame, his "red pod"—and it is here that he can capture the first sunlight of the morning to start his day. He softens the edges of the deck steps leading to this area with potted plants, ground cover and vintage finds.

Wells has perennials, bromeliads, and evergreen and deciduous trees in his design, but he confesses that he loves succulents most because of their foliage colors and texture. "They're pretty bulletproof and don't require much attention," he says, "but they give back so much. They're happy to shine on their own but play well with others."

In the pod area, he shows off a collection of red pots in different shapes. He recommends using plants with a common color theme and repeating plantings to help give a sense of continuity.

Wells likes to show off a variety of colors in his plantings, including plenty of green, with the odd dash of yellow. These shades also work well with old milk cans, tins, signs and even an old metal toy. "My yard is my sanctuary, my place to enjoy being creative and logical. It's where I find solitude and where I watch and learn. It's where I fill up my bucket in order to give at work and in life," he says.

1

1 **MAKE A STATEMENT** Timber steps lead to a neat little pod complete with a bench. It is framed by wood painted a bold red and shielded from other parts of the yard with timber and foliage screens. 2 **IN PLACE** A wooden shelving unit attached to a black-painted wooden fence is ideal for storing terra-cotta pots, logs and succulent arrangements. 3 **HARDY TRIO** Nestling in these terra-cotta pipes are succulents, a favorite since they don't need much water. Behind them is a cast-iron plant, which endures most growing conditions. 4 **OLD FINDS** This rustic corner is perfect for a collection of gardener's junk; Wells successfully marries vintage artifacts with storage items and plants. 5 **JUNKER'S EYE** Using his eye for detail, Wells found a new use for these metal containers.

Of all Wells' plants, succulents—with their hardiness and varying colors and textures—are his favorite.

BLACK BEAUTY This dark backdrop enhances the rusty containers and the different shades of green in the artfully staged succulents. OPPOSITE **FUN TIME** For younger visitors, Wells has incorporated a slide between levels.

1

1 **ROARING FIRE** When there's a chill, Wells just lights the logs in his firepit—set on a fireproof base to protect the deck—and sits on a lightweight gabion-basket stool to enjoy the glow. 2 **SHELF LIFE** This wooden shelving provides a great focal point for showing off backyard ornaments; it doubles as a storage space too. 3 **RUSTY DECOR** A timber screen is adorned with a rusty sign that has climbing plants entwined with it. 4 **3D LOOKS** It's such a great idea to create rustic, three-dimensional "picture boxes" out of odd bits of timber to display plants in colorful pots. 5 **GLOBE GLORY** Two wire hanging baskets have been clipped together to become a candleholder.

Get Inspired

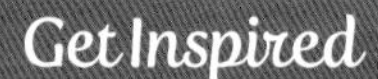

COUNTRY STRONG

Family influence is strong in this gorgeous country cabin, lovingly designed and built on a flower farm.

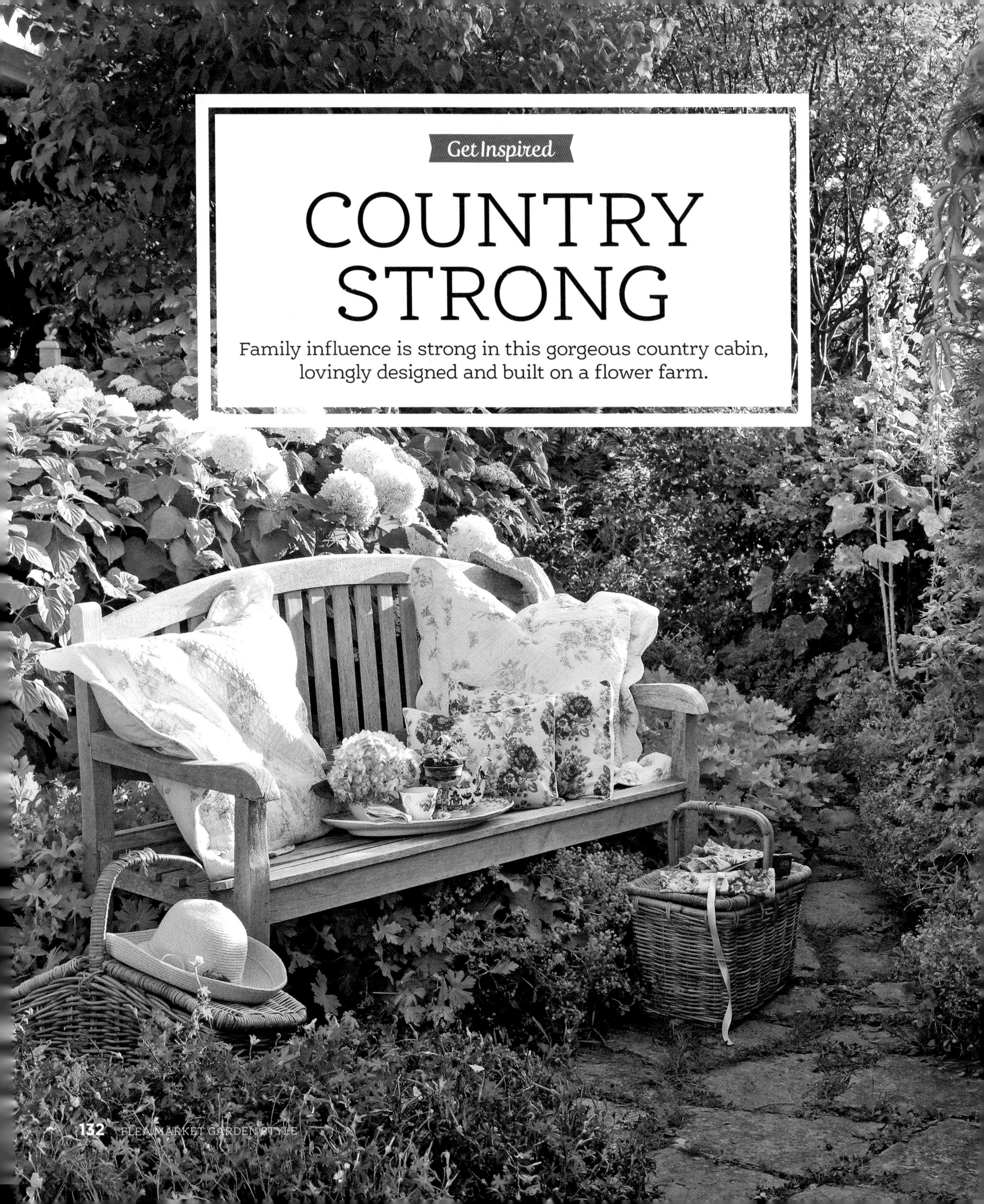

VINTAGE FINDS An old, painted chair on the porch is draped with cut hydrangeas and shaded by climbing hops. OPPOSITE **PICNIC SPOT** In a quiet corner of the yard, Michelle Bignell placed a delightful wooden bench in front of hydrangeas and a backdrop of trees.

1 **CRYSTAL SHIMMER** Bignell loves hanging old chandeliers outside; here, she added cut flowers in the outdoor shower. 2 **CURIOUS FELINE** Cats always know the best places to hang out—and this perch is the perfect spot in the shade. 3 **MOM'S THE WORD** A talented floral designer and stylist, Bignell is heavily influenced by both her mother's and grandmother's tastes. 4 **A TRANQUIL WASH** Shade-loving plants, such as lady's mantle, line the pathway to the outdoor shower shed.

For four generations, Michelle Bignell's family has worked the land of this country flower farm. So when she and husband Tom were offered the chance to build a family home here, they quickly seized the opportunity.

Using Michelle's talents as a stylist and floral designer, the couple scoured countless flea markets and auction houses and paired the items they found with family heirlooms and cherished vintage treasures.

The project has been a labor of love—and the completed effect is a rustic, shabby-chic beauty that's evident from the front porch to the timber outbuilding that serves as an outdoor shower for cooling off on a hot summer day while enjoying the view.

Reclaimed wood is used throughout, including for the floorboards—which tricks you into believing the home is much older than it really is. The garden is the stage for entertaining family and friends. "I use my yard for everything from simple tea parties to big dinner gatherings," says Bignell. "I take my cues from the landscape and use what I have on hand to create an unfussy outdoor oasis in keeping with our rural location." She favors meals where guests "can graze, taking a bite of this and a taste of that."

In Bignell's view, it's easy to create a welcoming setting: A pitcher of peonies or a bunch of lilacs (or something else in bloom at the time of year) is all that is needed to decorate the table, indoors or outdoors.

The scene—complete with a chandelier and vintage accessories—is set for outdoor dining.

1

1 **SEE THE LIGHT** A chandelier, suspended from a tree offering shade, hangs over the table. 2 **VINTAGE STYLE** Heirloom flatware contributes to the feel. 3 **FLORAL MAGIC** Bignell loves to use family linens to adorn her tea table; she marries them with vintage floral-patterned cups and saucers and cut flowers. 4 **FAIRY CAKES, YUM!** Who can resist these tasty treats decorated with mallow flowers? 5 **CHERRIES ON TOP** A vintage bowl holds fruit—just the thing for guests to snack on.

CHAPTER THREE

DIY GARDEN PROJECTS

Natural jute twine adds a rustic feel to your garden and is biodegradable (not to mention, it's very affordable!).

LIGHT UP YOUR YARD

Here's a bright idea! Don't throw your spent light bulbs into the trash—turn them into unique garden accessories.

We've all heard of a bulb vase, but these little beauties take that concept to the next level! The next time your light bulb flickers out, don't toss it in the trash. Instead, give it new life by turning it into a tiny hanging vase full of miniature blooms. Planning to host an outdoor party or dinner? Ask your family and friends to save their burnt-out bulbs for you. A yard filled with these homemade hangers will certainly impress your guests. Read on to learn how to make the unique vessel—it's surprisingly simple!

HOW TO MAKE IT

TIME 1 hour
COST $
MATERIALS

- Pliers
- Screw-base light bulbs
- Screwdriver or other pointy tool
- Jute twine for hanging (you'll need several feet per bulb)
- Small, delicate flowers

STEP 1 Using a pair of pliers, remove the small silver cap on the end of the light bulb. (This should just pull off.)
STEP 2 Inside the silver cap, you'll notice a small hole. Inside is a black glass section. Use a screwdriver to break this. Give it a wiggle and pull it out. (Keep the silver cap.)
STEP 3 Using the screwdriver, break the bulb's filament section and discard, leaving the bulb completely empty.
STEP 4 Tie the jute twine around the threaded (ribbed) part of the silver cap. Fill the glass bulb with water and replace the cap. Insert the flowers into the bulb, then hang it and admire your work!

Place feeders at least 30 feet away from large windows to prevent birds from accidentally flying into the glass.

IT'S SO TWEET!

Who doesn't love the sight—and sound—of birds visiting their yard? Let feathered friends know they're welcome to serenade you by making a feeder from a gourd!

One of the biggest draws of having a bird feeder in the yard is being able to watch all sorts of winged creatures flutter about when they come to visit. In the summer, their food is plentiful, but birds need all the help they can get come winter, when finding food can be a matter of life or death. Use our step-by-step instructions to make this gourd feeder designed to look like a bird and help these flying beauties survive. Be sure to clean out your feeder twice a week—moldy seeds can make birds sick.

1

2

3

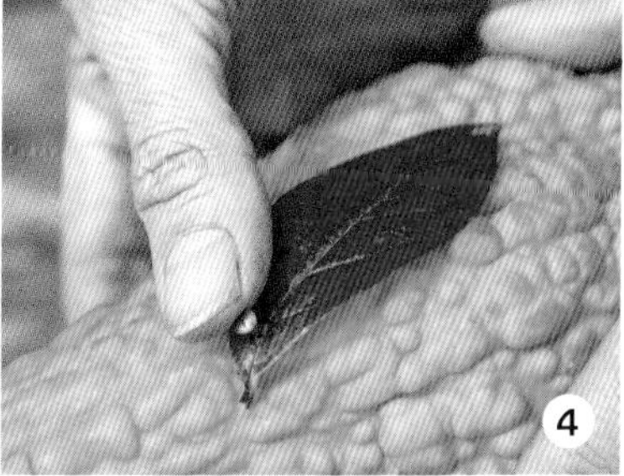

4

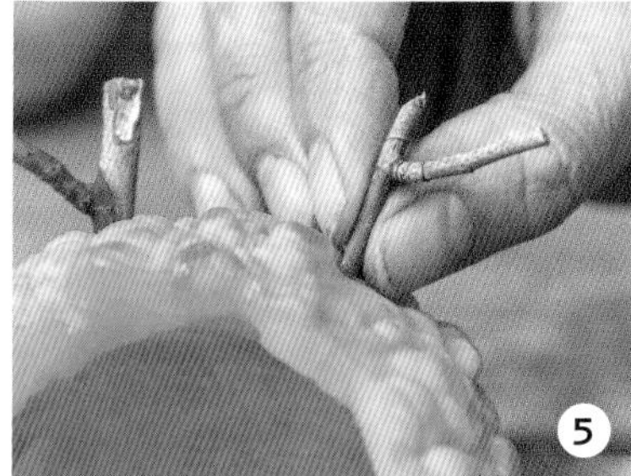

5

6

HOW TO MAKE IT

TIME 1 hour
COST $–$$
MATERIALS

- Drill with spade drill bits
- Dried gourd
- Spoon
- Rose hips (or berries), leaves and twigs
- Small nails or thumbtacks
- Skewer
- String, twine or wire

STEP 1 Using a drill with the spade-bit attachment, drill a large hole in the front of the gourd near the wide end.
STEP 2 Use a spoon to hollow out seeds and pith from gourd.
STEP 3 Using a smaller drill bit, make a hole on each side of the top of the gourd, big enough for the rose hips. Push them into place to make eyes.
STEP 4 Use small nails or thumbtacks to attach a leaf to each side for wings.
STEP 5 Force twigs into the base to create the feet.
STEP 6 Use a skewer to make a hole in the back of the gourd. Then thread a length of string or twine; knot the end inside. (If using wire, tie it around a twig instead.) Hang gourd and fill with birdseed.

Use the same checkerboard technique to decorate the rim of a much larger terra-cotta pot.

CHECKED OUT

With just a few bucks and 60 minutes of your time, you can make this marvelous mosaic-clad pot for yourself or as a gift for a loved one.

Tired of the same old pots you've been using year after year? Then it's time to give them a DIY makeover.

There's nothing square about this homemade checkerboard-style pot! Put any leftover bathroom tiles you have stored in the garage to good use. Don't have any? No worries—you can pick some up at your local home-improvement or crafts store. They're inexpensive—plus, that way, you get to choose the color scheme to match where you want to put the planter. It's a great pot for your indoor plants.

1

2

3

4

5

6

HOW TO MAKE IT

TIME 1 hour (active time)
COST $
MATERIALS
- Wooden ice cream sticks
- Ready-mixed tile adhesive grout
- Matte ceramic pot (to help adhesive stick)
- Small square tiles (test the size to make sure they're not too large to fit the pot)
- Sponge and damp cloth
- Matching decorative stones (if required for the rim)

STEP 1 Use a wooden stick to apply a thick layer of adhesive to the outside of the pot.
STEP 2 Press tiles on sides of the pot, alternating colors and leaving an equal gap between tiles; let set overnight.
STEP 3 Use another stick to spread the grout to fill the gaps between the tiles.
STEP 4 Using a sponge, go over all gaps to ensure that they are filled with grout.
STEP 5 Remove the excess grout from the tile surface with a damp cloth.
STEP 6 If the pot's rim is visible at the upper edge, apply a layer of adhesive to secure stones over it.

An ombré effect begins with one color and moves into another, like these blue-to-green wings.

WINGING WAYS

Creating these vibrant, decorative dragonflies is a fun and super-easy craft to do with children of all ages.

Kids have been having fun with sycamore and maple seeds, also known as polly noses, for years, opening them up and sticking them on their noses for some silly fun. Well, here's another more aesthetically pleasing way to delight in the helicopter-like seeds: Turn them into beautiful dragonflies. They're so simple to make and a great creative project to do with children—even young ones, with proper supervision. And the expedition to collect the sycamore seeds can be just as fun as the craft itself!

1

2

3

4

HOW TO MAKE IT

TIME 1 hour (active time)
COST $
MATERIALS

- Craft paint: 2 blue shades, 2 green shades and white
- Fine paintbrush
- Scrap of paper
- Sycamore or maple seeds (2 for each dragonfly)
- 2 twigs (1 for each body)
- Hot-glue gun and glue sticks

STEP 1 Practice blending paint colors on a scrap of paper to create a gradient of shades.
STEP 2 Break each seed down the center, forming 2 "wings" with seed pods. Paint each wing with lighter, then darker, shades of blue or green, creating an ombré effect.
STEP 3 Break a twig to 4 inches long; paint it in the darkest hue used on the wings. Once wings and body are dry, use a hot-glue gun to attach wings to twig.
STEP 4 Paint and assemble second dragonfly in another shade, following steps 2 and 3. Let the glue dry thoroughly before hanging outdoors or in.

For a never-ending supply of willow, grow your own. Cut a few first-year rods and use them for crafts.

LAND A FISH

It's amazing how you can create stunning ornaments for the home or garden out of the raw materials you find in your yard. This decoration is quite a catch!

Here's a project to satisfy the dream-weaver in all of us. Willow branches are a great material to use because they're so flexible. Be sure to harvest branches from first-year growth, since they are generally the most pliable. (Second- and third-year branches become stronger and are harder to work with.) Look for rods that are long and thin with a consistent diameter. If you can bend the willow branch around your wrist without it breaking, you can weave it into a fish! Follow our simple instructions to create your own backyard decor.

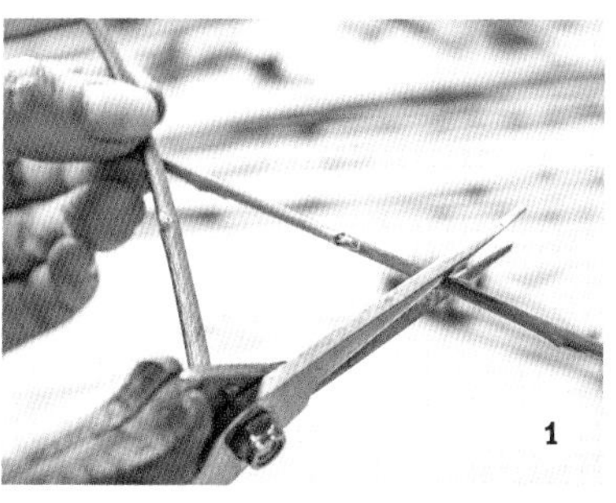
1

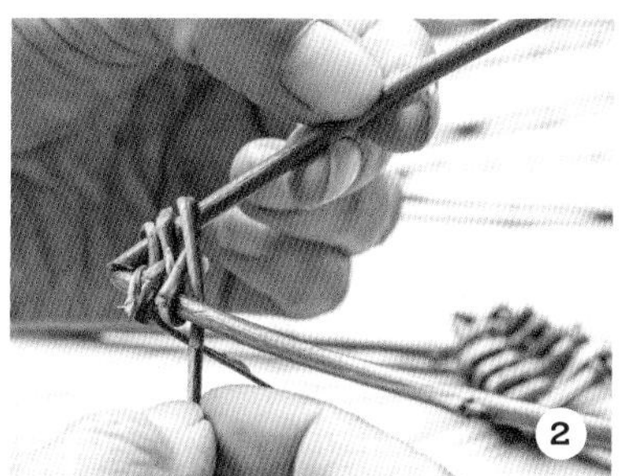
2

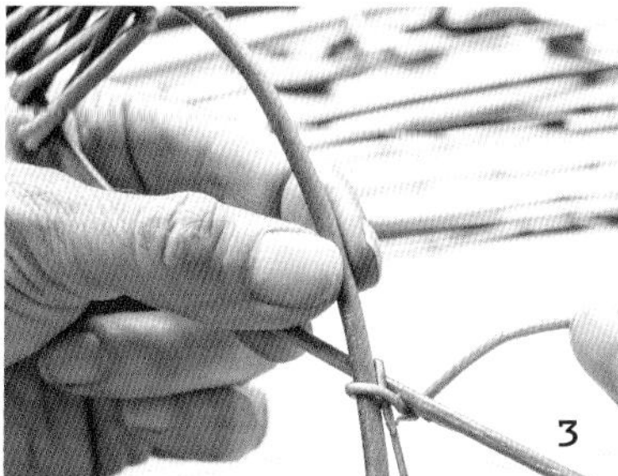
3

4

5

6

HOW TO MAKE IT

TIME 1 hour
COST $
MATERIALS

- Scissors or pruning shears
- About 6 feet of thin, pliable willow (for the fish)
- 6 feet of very thin, pliable willow (for weaving and tying)

STEP 1 Trim any branching from the thin willow and bend it in half, making a point to form the fish's nose. Cross the opposite ends about 6 inches from the ends to form the tail.
STEP 2 Starting at the nose, weave the very thin willow back and forth around the thin willow to form the head. Cut off remaining willow and tuck in the ends.
STEP 3 Tie a piece of very thin willow around the ends where they cross at the tail end.
STEP 4 Weave thin willow between the tail pieces and tuck in the ends.
STEP 5 Trim the ends of the tail.
STEP 6 Think of creative ways to display your artwork, like from a bendy willow fishing rod (opposite page), or craft a whole school of fish.

If you plan on keeping the ladybugs and bees outside, finish them with a weatherproof clear varnish.

BUZZWORTHY FUN

Stuck inside on a rainy day? This easy garden project can be done indoors with kids and used outside when the sun is shining.

The next time you pay a visit to the park or beach with the kids, make sure you add stone collecting to your list of activities. Look for smooth, flat rocks that are roughly the size of your hand or smaller. Bring them home and save them for a rainy day, when you need some entertainment with a fun garden craft. Follow our guide here or use your imagination to create all sorts of creatures. And when the rain clears, you can use your rock bugs to decorate the garden or simply to play some tic-tac-toe!

HOW TO MAKE IT

TIME 1 hour (active time)
COST $
MATERIALS

- Smooth, flat stones
- Fine paintbrush
- Acrylic paints: red, yellow, black and white
- Varnish

STEP 1 Wash and dry the stones, then paint each either red (ladybug) or yellow (bee).
STEP 2 Once they're dry (you can use a hair dryer if you don't want to wait too long), use black to paint on the heads and other markings. Use white to paint on eyes, wings and antennae. Let dry, then finish with a coat of varnish to protect them from the elements.
STEP 3 Plant them in the garden, or use chalk to create an outdoor tic-tac-toe board and play away!

TIP Want to speed up the process of making rock bugs? Instead of collecting the stones, you can buy landscape rocks from a garden store.

Move your container to an area that gets partial shade on sunny or hot summer days.

FRAME IT

Give flowering annuals a place to climb in a container garden with the help of a naturally elegant willow frame.

Climbers are usually trained to go up a trellis. But why not try something out of the ordinary, like this DIY frame?

Given the right support, climbing and trailing plants will reward you with an outstanding display of blooms. This project will help you provide support to a beautiful purple bell vine by using lengths of fresh willow woven to form a dome-shaped frame for it to climb up. Plant it with trailing lobelia that spills over the edges and hides the potting soil. Use a flea market find like a metal wash basin or galvanized pot as a planter.

1

2

3

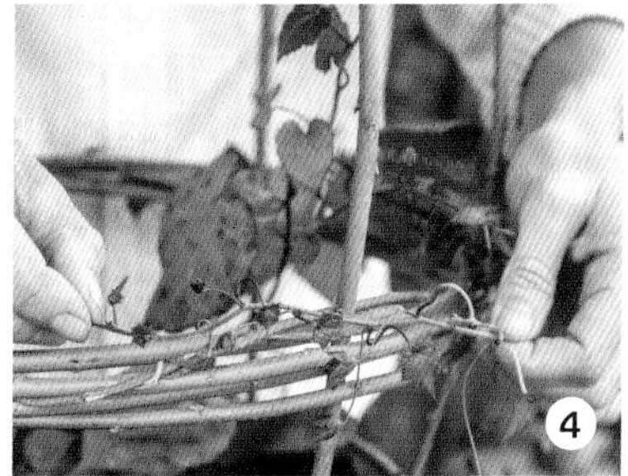
4

5

6

HOW TO MAKE IT

TIME 1 hour
COST $–$$
MATERIALS

- Metal wash basin or galvanized pot
- Potting soil
- Purple bell vine plants
- Eight 4- to 5-foot lengths of fresh willow, leaves stripped
- Lobelia 'Trailing Red' plants

STEP 1 Partially fill the basin with potting soil. Place the purple bell vine in the center, then add potting soil around it, firming the soil.
STEP 2 Bury one end of one willow branch in the soil. Bend it to form an arch and bury the other end. Repeat with two more branches, spacing them evenly.
STEP 3 Weave other branches horizontally through sides of the structure to make it more sturdy and provide support.
STEP 4 Thread tendrils of the purple bell vine through the horizontal willow branches.
STEP 5 Underplant with lobelia, pointing the young plants outward.
STEP 6 Water the soil frequently and occasionally use a liquid fertilizer.

Herbal remedies have a long history, but check with your doctor before taking anything new.

MEDICINAL MAGIC

If you prefer to look for natural remedies for minor ailments, try out this recipe for a beautiful homegrown first-aid box.

Many herbs have both culinary and medicinal uses. Take calendula—the petals are edible and make a great addition to salads, and the plant has been used as an anti-inflammatory. Purple sage, which has been used to treat fevers, colds and coughs, also adds a savory flavor to butter for a delicious pasta sauce and can be used in any recipe that calls for common sage. There's even a third benefit to creating a medicinal herb garden—it's pretty to look at, especially when planted in a rustic wooden box.

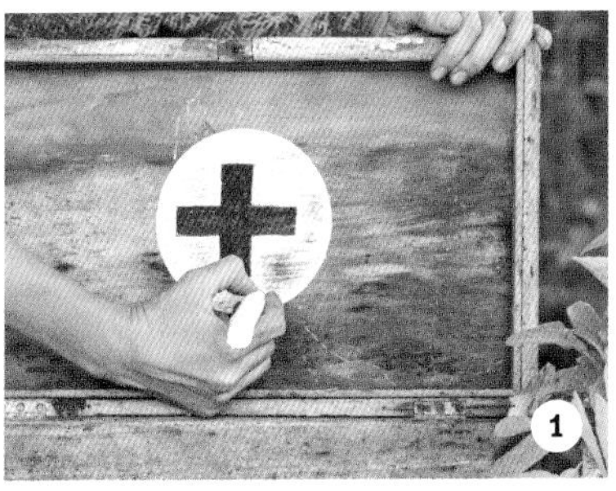
1

2

3

4

5

6

HOW TO MAKE IT

TIME 1 hour
COST $$
MATERIALS

- Red and white markers
- Pot (to trace circle)
- Wooden suitcase-style box
- Garden trowel or scoop
- Gravel
- Potting soil
- Medicinal-herb plants: comfrey, calendula, purple sage, feverfew, creeping thyme, Eastern coneflower, aloe vera, California nettle

STEP 1 Use a white marker to trace the outer edge of the pot inside the box lid. Draw a red cross centered in the circle. Fill rest of the circle in white.
STEP 2 Add a layer of gravel to the bottom of the box to provide drainage.
STEP 3 Fill the box with potting soil, stopping 2 inches from the top.
STEP 4 Plant the largest herbs first, then the smaller plants.
STEP 5 Add more potting soil to the box and firm the plants into the soil.
STEP 6 Top with a layer of gravel. Water the box regularly and wait to see the flowers burst open.

Even if you're trying to achieve a rustic look, sand the pallet before turning it into a planter. No one likes a splinter!

PEEK-A-BOO

Who would've guessed a simple wooden pallet could be used as a vertical planter? This is a great afternoon project to create an easy-to-care-for succulent display.

This super-easy idea provides a rustic look in your yard. Wooden pallets are inexpensive at home-improvement stores (and local garden, grocery and pet stores may even toss them out). We've used succulents here. They don't need much watering and tolerate poor-quality soil, so you can reuse last year's potting soil from your patio containers. Succulent displays are perfect for people who don't have lots of time for regular plant care. If you have the time, you could use annuals or salad leaves and herbs, too—just remember to water them frequently.

HOW TO MAKE IT

TIME 2 hours
COST $$
MATERIALS
- Wooden pallet
- Wood blocks or planks to cover sides and back of pallet
- Hand saw, ruler and pencil
- Hammer and nails
- Scissors
- Burlap cloth
- Heavy-duty stapler and staples
- Potting soil
- Succulents

STEP 1 Place pallet facedown on a flat surface. Fill the gaps on the pallet's sides with blocks of wood or planks, cutting to fit if needed; leave the top end of the pallet open.
STEP 2 Secure blocks by hammering in nails diagonally.
STEP 3 Cut enough burlap to fully line the inside of the pallet front. Staple in place.
STEP 4 Fill the pallet with soil.
STEP 5 Place planks over pallet, adding soil between wood and burlap; nail in place.
STEP 6 Lift the pallet upright and add more potting soil via open top end. Cut small holes in burlap and plant your succulents inside.

Try potting different varieties of the same plant, such as thyme (shown here) or pick several types for dramatic contrast.

WHEEL DEAL

Give this neat little rustic planter a whirl—it's a clever way to separate varieties of the same plant or try a few contrasting versions.

Wagon wheels hearken back to earlier days, but their homespun appeal is timeless. You can often find them at yard sales and flea markets, but decorative versions are also available online. They also serve a practical purpose in this planter: The spokes in the wheels help keep the plants from infringing on their neighbors. You'll still need a base to hold the soil and keep your plants together. Our version here uses a galvanized metal tub to maintain that bucolic look.

1

2

3

4

5

6

HOW TO MAKE IT

TIME 1 hour
COST $$
MATERIALS

- Round, galvanized metal washtub or other container
- Drill and drill bits
- Gravel
- Potting soil
- Wooden wheel
- Variety of plants
- Permanent marker
- Wooden plant-labeling sticks

STEP 1 If the washtub doesn't have drainage holes, drill a few holes in the bottom, then add a layer of gravel.
STEP 2 Fill the tub with potting soil, leaving enough room at the top for the wheel and plants.
STEP 3 Put the wheel on top.
STEP 4 Lay out the types of plants to decide where they will go, making sure the colors coordinate.
STEP 5 Insert your plants into the tub, then firm them in, adding additional potting soil where required.
STEP 6 Use the marker to write the names of the plants on labels. Place them in the soil so you'll know which plant is which when they sprout!

To prevent your veggies from drying out over an open flame, coat them with a little olive oil before grilling.

FIRE IN THE HOLE

This build-a-barbecue firepit is so easy. It takes very little time and won't break the bank. You'll be grilling within an hour of building!

Building your very own firepit is easier than it looks. It's a great addition to your yard—you can use it for cooking and to keep warm and cozy on a chilly evening.

Before building, check local town codes to ensure compliance. Then figure out the best place for your firepit: Don't put it too close to your house, or a neighbor's, and steer clear of any low-hanging trees, which may present a fire hazard. When the work is done, set up some chairs and enjoy the warm glow and freshly grilled food.

1

2

3

4

HOW TO MAKE IT

TIME 1 hour
COST $$
MATERIALS

- Paving slab (at least 18 inches square)
- About 40 bricks
- 2 metal grates—1 smaller for charcoal; 1 larger for cooking
- Kindling or firelighters
- Charcoal

STEP 1 Place paving slab at desired firepit location. Use the diameter of the smaller metal grate as a guide to position bricks to form three-quarters of a circle.
STEP 2 Add two more layers in the same pattern, decreasing the size slightly with each layer to create a ledge. Rest the small grate on ledge. Add two more layers of bricks on top to form a cooking-grate ledge. Leave a ventilation hole at the back.
STEP 3 Place kindling or firelighters on bottom grate and light it.
STEP 4 Add charcoal. When it turns ash gray, place large grate on top to grill food (see main image).

Prevent wooden handles on garden tools from becoming dull and splintered by applying a coat of linseed oil.

STYLISH STORAGE

Follow this fabulous project to transform an old freestanding bookcase into a smart outdoor depository.

If you scour garage sales, flea markets and thrift stores, you may realize that there are so many ways to repurpose someone else's unwanted items. It just takes a bit of imagination and ingenuity.

With a fresh coat of waterproof paint, this old bookshelf makes an attractive addition to your garden, and a convenient space to store tools and dry your fresh herbs. Attaching Mason jars to the underside of the shelf adds an unexpected touch of whimsy—plus, it eliminates the threat of the glass jars tipping over.

1

2

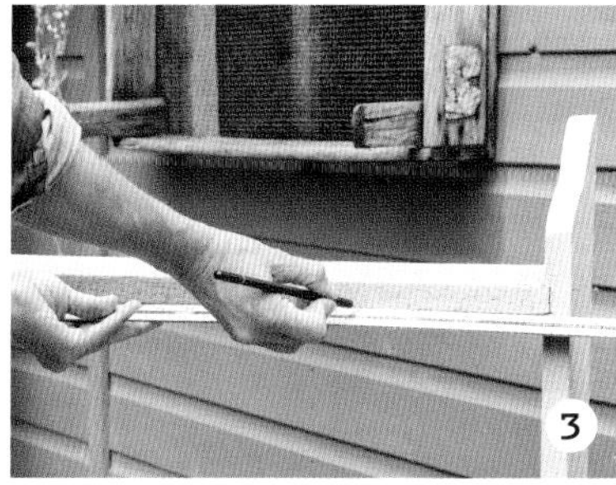
3

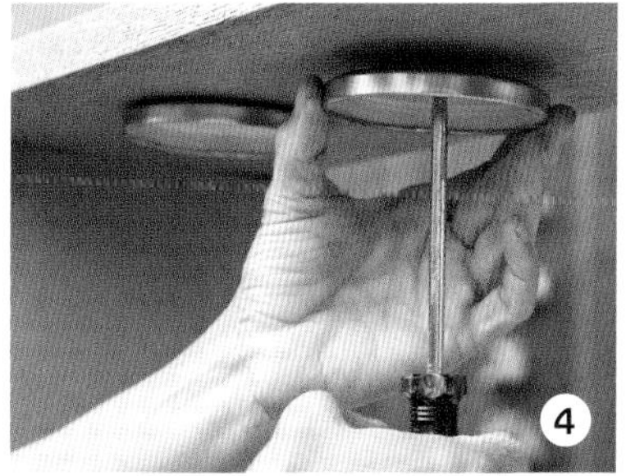
4

5

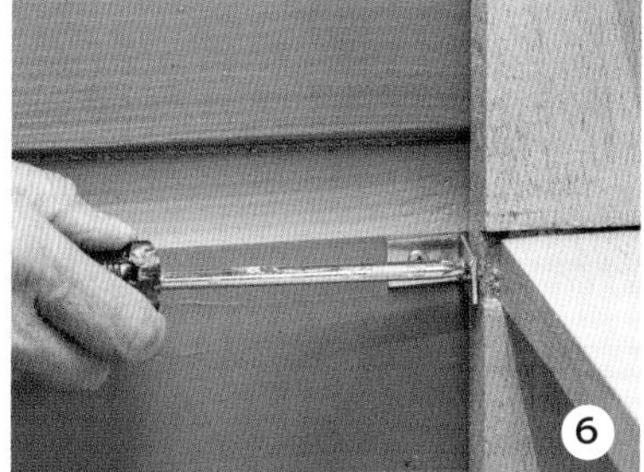
6

HOW TO MAKE IT

TIME 5 hours
COST $$
MATERIALS

- Wooden bookcase
- Water-resistant paint
- Paintbrush
- 4 Mason jars with lids
- Awl
- Tape measure and pencil
- Screws
- Screwdriver
- About 10 cup hooks
- Six zinc-plated corner braces (optional)

STEP 1 Protect work surface with newspaper. Apply several coats of paint to the bookcase, letting the paint dry thoroughly after each coat.
STEP 2 Place jar lids on a hard surface, then use awl to pierce a hole in the center of each lid.
STEP 3 Measure and mark the placement of the lids on the underside of the top shelf, spacing them evenly.
STEP 4 Screw a lid to each mark, then screw on the jars.
STEP 5 Screw cup hooks into the shelf edges to hang tools.
STEP 6 If desired, use corner braces to attach shelf against a wall to keep steady. You could also attach it flush.

Easily switch up your seasonal decor by placing a table runner over a simple white tablecloth.

SPREAD CHEER

These simple pompoms, made out of tissue paper, help brighten any outdoor space and pair perfectly with paper lanterns or other lights.

Set the tone for a fun and festive alfresco dinner with paper pompoms. These carnation-like decorations are so easy and inexpensive to make and will add a cheerful elegance to your tablescape. Our table features whites and blues, but you can use any color tissue paper to match any theme—such as pink and blue for a baby shower, or red, white and blue for Independence Day—the options are limitless.

Add to the ethereal vibe with a string of tiny white lights and some tea lights on your table.

HOW TO MAKE IT

TIME 1 hour
COST $
MATERIALS

- Tissue paper (6 sheets for each pompom)
- Thread to match paper
- Scissors and ruler

STEP 1 Unfold and layer three sheets of tissue paper. Holding all three sheets together, fold up a $1^1/_2$-inch strip on one edge as shown.
STEP 2 Flip the stack over to the other side and fold over again, making accordion folds. Repeat until you reach the end. Unfold, layer and accordion-fold the remaining three sheets of tissue paper in the same way, so you end up with two folded strips.
STEP 3 Layer the strips and tie securely in the middle with thread, leaving two long lengths for hanging later.
STEP 4 Trim the ends in curves as shown.
STEP 5 Separate layers one at a time, fluffing them up to form a rounded, pompom shape.
STEP 6 Tie the thread ends together to form a hanging loop for the pompom. Hang from string lights or branches.

Turn the top of your birdhouse into a living roof to add greenery to your feathered friends' home.

FOR THE BIRDS

Living—or green—roofs are a big trend in houses across the globe, so why not try a scaled-down version for your backyard garden?

Ready-made wooden birdhouses are easy to find at crafts stores or gardening shops. Do a basic paint job one better by transforming the roof of the house into an attractive planter that will draw rave reviews along with visits from those flying by. Bonus: A living roof helps to keep the house—and your feathered friends—cooler during the summer heat. Hardy succulents make a nice topper for this house, but you can also use perennials such as low-growing sedums, which are easy to care for and attract bees along with the birds!

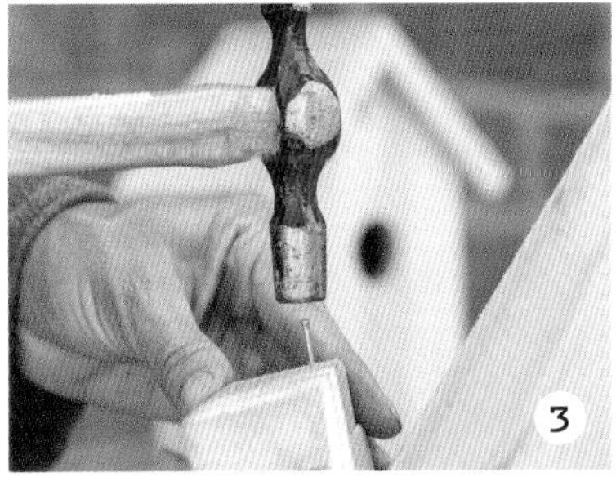

HOW TO MAKE IT

TIME 1 hour (active time)
COST $–$$
MATERIALS

- Ready-made wooden birdhouse
- Pen and ruler
- Saw
- 6 short lengths of wood (about 12 inches or less)
- Hammer
- Nails
- Sandpaper
- Paintbrush
- Wood stain, varnish or paint
- Potting soil
- Assorted succulents

STEP 1 Find a solid work surface (outdoors, if possible).
STEP 2 Measure the outer edge of the roof; mark and cut the lengths of wood to match, allowing for pieces to meet at each corner so they'll hold soil.
STEP 3 Nail the wood pieces to the birdhouse. Sand edges.
STEP 4 Stain, varnish or paint your birdhouse, letting dry after each coat.
STEP 5 Add soil to top of house, then place succulents in the soil, firming roots.
STEP 6 Hang birdhouse as desired,nailing or hooking it to a wall or tree.

Hang these cans from a piece of twine that runs between tree branches or across your yard.

SIMPLE GARDEN GLOWS

Turn metal cans from pantry goods into decorative lanterns that will cast a lovely light anywhere you place them.

Forget the recycling bin: Start saving those food cans to transform them into low-cost decorative tea-light holders. Simply clean, wash and set them aside for when you are ready.

You can create patterns of your choosing, from stars and flowers to snowflakes or simple geometric motifs. Cut a piece of note or graph paper to fit the can, and wrap it around to determine the best size and placement of the motifs. Sketch your motif(s) and use the paper as a reusable template. Try repeating the motif on both sides of the can.

1

2

3

HOW TO MAKE IT

TIME 1 hour (active time)
COST $
MATERIALS

- Tin cans, washed and labels removed
- Masking tape
- Templates for desired motifs
- Hammer
- Nails in assorted thicknesses
- Wire cutters
- Spool of 18-gauge wire
- Tea lights

STEP 1 Fill cans with water and freeze until solid. (This will help the can hold its shape when making the holes.) Then gather remaining materials.
STEP 2 Once it's frozen, place a can on its side; tape the template to the side. Hammer nail into can to create holes along template lines. Also make two holes opposite each other just below the can's rim.
STEP 3 Remove ice. Cut about 12 inches of wire; pass ends through the holes on the rim. Bend wire ends to secure, forming a hanging loop. Place a tea light inside and hang where desired.

Use old sheets or other bedding, or check out a sewing or crafts store to find your fabrics.

POINT THE WAY TO THE PARTY

This simple how-to needs only a little sewing yet produces great results for your celebration.

Bunting is said to have originated around the turn of the 17th century, when the British Royal Navy used woolen fabric and ribbon to make flags displayed for pomp and circumstance. Pennant flags have since been adopted universally as something that indicates a celebration. They're an inexpensive way to transform your yard or deck, or wherever you entertain, and can be used year-round. Design your own flags to decorate any outside area and give your garden a colorful, festive lift with fabrics you can find in a craft store or flea market.

1

2

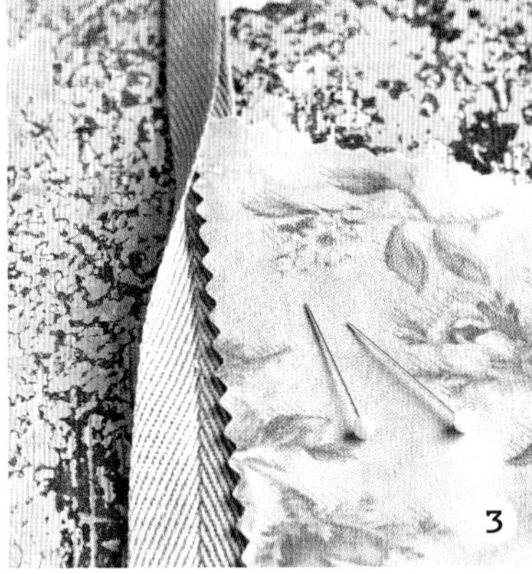
3

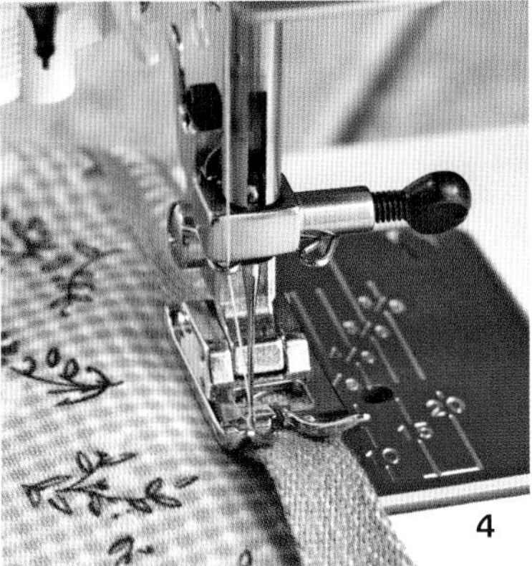
4

HOW TO MAKE IT

TIME 1 hour
COST $
MATERIALS

- Cotton fabrics in desired prints
- Pencil and ruler
- Lightweight cardboard
- Scissors (to cut cardboard)
- Scallop-edge rotary cutter or pinking shears
- Double-fold bias binding and matching thread
- Straight pins
- Sewing machine

STEP 1 Choose several complementary fabrics.
STEP 2 Mark and cut out desired flag shape from cardboard to make template. Place the template on the fabric and, using a rotary cutter, cut around it. (Scalloped/pinked edges don't ravel, so there's no need to hem.)
STEP 3 Open out desired length of bias binding. Insert flags, evenly spaced, between binding layers; fold down top layer and pin in place.
STEP 4 Stitch the flags in place, then hang as desired.

You can add on your own accessories or decor —simply use your imagination!

KEEPING WATCH

A whimsical "bucket lady" scarecrow uses simple, everyday items to create a backyard sentry that will keep uninvited feathered visitors away.

A well-placed scarecrow is a time-honored way to scare off birds who may feast on the berries and seeds in your yard. You can easily buy premade scarecrows, but it's a lot more fun to make your own. We often think of the figure as a male, but females can certainly make the mark, as in our playful bucket lady. Choose any plants you want: In our model, we used bloodleaf and switchgrass to form her hair, then placed creeping zinnia to fill in the middle portion and creeping Charlie to trail elegantly down her CD-framed skirt.

1

2

3

HOW TO MAKE IT

TIME 1–2 hours (active time)
COST $
MATERIALS

- Hammer
- Pole or old broomstick
- Drill with pole-sized drill bit
- 3 large galvanized buckets
- Nails
- Potting soil
- Wire cutters
- String
- Old CDs
- Tent pegs
- 1 length of wood (for arms)
- Paint and paintbrushes
- Plants (see intro)

STEP 1 Hammer pole into ground. Drill a hole in bottom of each bucket; thread two buckets onto pole. Hammer a nail into pole below each bucket to secure. Fill with soil.
STEP 2 Attach strings to the pole above bottom bucket. Slip CDs onto strings. Weave additional strings horizontally. Anchor to ground with pegs.
STEP 3 Nail wood to pole above second bucket. Paint a face on third bucket; let dry. Fill with potting soil; add plants to all.

Elevate the look by selecting a single shade—in this case plum—to unite the various elements.

DIY Garden Projects

CRATE EXPECTATIONS

Add ample storage (and flea market appeal!) to your yard with artfully arranged wooden crates.

No storage? No problem! This easy project marries pretty and practical with garden-storage-meets-art-installation appeal. An odd number of crates works best for creating compelling visual impact, but feel free to collect a variety of crates in different shapes, sizes and materials. A well-balanced layout often includes a mix of various heights, widths and depths. Fill the crates with potted flowers and plants, or gather a collection of some of your favorite flea market finds with an eclectic air.

HOW TO MAKE IT

TIME 2 hours
COST $
MATERIALS

- Wooden crates
- Exterior paint or sealer
- Paintbrush
- $1\frac{1}{2}$-inch exterior wood screws (for metal or brick installations, may need metal or masonry screws)
- Drill and bits

STEP 1 Get a collection of assorted sturdy crates.

STEP 2 Seal crates with paint or sealer; paint insides first. Let each layer dry before applying the next.

STEP 3 Position into desired layout; take a picture for reference. Using wood screws (or masonry or metal screws, depending on surface), use a drill to attach first crate to exterior surface. Drill one screw into each corner of the crate. Referring to the photo, repeat until each crate is securely attached to exterior surface.

STEP 4 Dress each crate with the items you wish to display.

To keep cut flowers alive longer, add 3 tablespoons of sugar and 2 tablespoons of white vinegar to each quart of water.

BRIGHT, BIG & BEAUTIFUL

You can't beat homegrown blooms, so show them off as a hand-tied arrangement with these expert tips. It's easier than you think!

Colorful, bold blossoms look great in an arrangement—and you don't need to shell out big bucks at the florist for one. Our top tip is to keep it simple and follow this one rule: Group large flowers together in a low vase. This creates a balanced, polished-looking centerpiece. If you're going for a special look for a garden party or other fancy affair, try creating a centerpiece of multiple arrangements, like in the photo at left. Place several smaller vases—with just a few blooms in each—around the larger bouquet. Place bouquets in a cool spot.

1

2

3

4

HOW TO MAKE IT

TIME 30 minutes
COST $
MATERIALS
- Scissors
- Backyard flowers (such as dahlias, sneezeweed, montbretia and seed heads of castor oil plants)
- Jute or natural raffia twine
- Vase

STEP 1 Trim stems of each flower to about a foot long (they'll be trimmed to fit the vase later). Cut off lower leaves.
STEP 2 Hold a larger bloom loosely by its stem, under the petals, and keep adding others to your hand one by one. The closer under the flowers you hold the stems, the tighter the round of the bouquet will be.
STEP 3 Add in smaller blooms in complementary colors around the large flowers. Once happy with the arrangement, wrap and tie twine around the stems where your hand was.
STEP 4 Cut stem ends on an angle so they're shorter than the depth of the vase. Fill vase with water; add flowers.

Tropical plants are known to get thirsty! Use a pot with a saucer that will retain water to keep soil moist.

TROPICAL DREAM

If you want to bring an exotic splash to your garden, try this planting recipe, which promises to deliver months of vibrant color.

Who doesn't want to feel like they're at a five-star resort while relaxing in their own backyard? An arrangement of colorful tropical plants can turn your space into a garden paradise. It can be tough to know which blooms will look good together when often all you can see when shopping is their foliage. This planting recipe will provide you with a stunning tropical combination. Don't forget to use the tallest plants ("thrillers") at the back, your medium-sized plants ("fillers") just beneath, and your trailing plant ("spillers") below.

1

2

3

4

HOW TO MAKE IT

TIME 1 hour
COST $$
MATERIALS
- Container
- Potting soil
- Bolivian begonia 'Santa Cruz Sunset'
- Begonia 'Glowing Embers'
- Gold licorice plants
- Cherry pie plant 'Butterfly Kisses'
- Bright Ideas series black sweet potato vine plants
- Parrot's beak plants

STEP 1 Fill container with potting soil, stopping 5 inches below the rim. Take begonias out of their pots and sink them into the soil toward the center of the container.
STEP 2 Plant remaining flowers (first "fillers" and then "spillers" around the edge).
STEP 3 Top off the soil and firm in the plants.
STEP 4 Gently water and wait for tropical planter to reward you with fantastic blooms! If potting soil doesn't contain slow-release fertilizer, feed regularly with liquid fertilizer.

Adding a layer of organic or plastic mulch to your plants can help prevent tomatoes from cracking.

GARDEN CANDY

Try this aptly named sweet delight that's easy to grow and loaded with important nutrients (not sugar).

A packet of Garden Candy seeds contains three types of cherry tomatoes: Sweet Gold F1, Supersweet 100 F1 and Sungold F1. With three such vibrant colors, they're bound to look as great on your plate as they'll taste. The bite-size beauties are easy to grow and produce an early and abundant harvest. They make a great snack right off the vine and are the perfect accompaniment for your homegrown salad. To ensure they're well watered, invest in inexpensive plastic water rings. You can use them again year after year.

1

2

3

4

5

6

HOW TO MAKE IT

TIME 1.5–2 hours (active time)
COST $$
MATERIALS

- Garden Candy seeds
- Terra-cotta pots (1 large; 3 small)
- Potting soil
- Tomato grow bags
- Three watering rings
- Scissors or knife
- 9 bamboo canes
- Twine

STEP 1 Fill large pot with soil, then sprinkle a few seeds on top. Add a fine layer of soil to cover seeds and firm down.
STEP 2 Once seedlings develop a second set of leaves, carefully replant into the small pots.
STEP 3 When plants are 5 to 6 inches tall, they're ready to transplant. Fill grow bags with soil. Cut three circles in bag to fit watering rings. Push rings into soil.
STEP 4 Fill centers of rings halfway with soil. Place one root ball in the center of each ring. Add more soil on top.
STEP 5 Place three canes in each ring. Secure at the top with twine; water plants.
STEP 6 Pick tomatoes as they ripen, and pinch side shoots.

DIY Garden Projects

10 MORE EASY IDEAS

Transform old junk into new treasures with these simple decorative garden displays.

1

1 **NIGHT BLOOMS** Pop floating tea lights into a water-filled galvanized tub and add your favorite flowers. (We chose dahlias.) 2 **LADDER 2.0** Bring an old ladder to life—position it horizontally on a wall and use it as a shelf to hold ornaments. 3 **STRUNG ALONG** Old funnels make perfect string holders; you'll never need to bother with undoing tangles. 4 **CRUSH IT** Create outdoor artwork with tin cans: Squash them, pierce them through the center, thread them on thick wire and enjoy their rustic beauty. 5 **PERFECT RECALL** Remove the dial from an old phone, replace the innards with potting soil and plant succulents within.

6 **LIGHT IT UP** Thread terra-cotta pots onto bamboo canes; secure with elastic and ribbons. Fill with fine gravel and add tea lights. 7 **COLANDER CURIOSITY** Put a liner in an old colander; plant your favorite kitchen herbs and hang outside your back door. 8 **BAGGAGE SURPRISE** An old suitcase can be a unique special-occasion holder for gifts at a wedding or bar mitzvah. 9 **PLATE DESIGN** Create a mosaic on a terra-cotta saucer with bits of colored crockery; adhere the pieces with ready-mix adhesive grout. 10 **PERFECT STAGE** Use an old hutch as outdoor shelving for small potted plants; you can keep your pruning shears in the drawers!

10

A
African-styled backyard retreat, 10–11
Alfresco dining spaces
  lighting for, 70–73
  repurposed shipping container as, 59
  styles and ideas, 64–67, 136
  table decor for, 64, 68–69, 84, 86–87, 104, 164
  in urban oasis, 90–93
Alpine plants, for miniature gardens, 76–77
Arbor, modern, with seating pod, 125, 126

B
Backyard retreats
  with African theme, 10–11
  development over time, 22–23
  eclectic style, 19
  English style, 15
  industrial metal pieces in, 20–21
  industrial-styled, 20–21
  modern style, 14
  romantic vintage, 10–11
  seaside-styled, 16–17
  whimsical, 18
Bamboo privacy screen, 123
Barbecue firepit, how to build, 160–161
Bedsprings, as climbing plant support, 50
Bee decorations, how to make, 150–151
Benches
  in country cabin garden, 132
  potting/display, 38–41
Bignell, Michelle, country cabin retreat of, 132–137
Bird feeders, gourd, how to make, 142–143
Birdhouses
  grouped display, 114
  individual styles, 42–46
  with living roof, how to make, 166–167
  as planters, 47
  primitive, 105
Bookcase, making outdoor storage from, 162–163
Bottles, colored, building walls with, 29
Breezeway, sitting area in, 116–117
Brick pavers, 110, 115, 119, 120
Bucket lady sculpture, how to make, 172–173
Buckets, galvanized, 99, 127
Bunting
  fabric, how to make, 170–171
  floral, 50

C
Candelabra, for alfresco dining, 65
Candles/Candleholders
  for alfresco dining, 65, 70–73
  battery-operated, 68, 72, 74
  floating, 74, 182
  wire-basket globe, 131
Canopy
  tablecloth used as, 74
  vintage lace used as, 87
  of wisteria, 66
CDs, for bucket lady sculpture, 172–173
Chairs
  decorative use of, 133
  as focal points, 98
  for plant display, 108
  as planters, 18, 32
Chandeliers
  for alfresco dining, 136
  in outdoor shower, 134
  planters on, 33
  wagon-wheel, for hanging planters, 31
Cherry tomatoes, how to grow, 180–181
Chic style. *See* Shabby-chic decor
Children
  miniature gardens for, 78–79
  slide for, between garden levels, 129
China cups, repurposing as planters, 32, 34–37
Climbing plants, frames/support for, 18, 24–25, 49, 50, 53, 109, 124, 131, 133, 152
  making from willow branches, how-to, 152–153
Clothespins, as fence around miniature garden, 78
Coastal-styled backyard retreat, 16–17
Colander, as hanging herb planter, 184
Colors
  for African-styled backyard retreat, 10–11
  dark exterior wall, as garden backdrop, 121, 128
  eye-catching fabric, in repurposed shed, 63
  for modern backyard retreat, 14
  for modern garden shed, 59
  royal blue accents, 106–114, 119
  use in multitiered backyard, 123, 125, 129, 131
  for whimsical backyard retreat, 18
  for wooden crate storage modules, 174–175
Containers. *See also* Planters, ideas for; Terra-cotta pots/saucers; *specific types of containers*
  in breezeway, 116–117
  making willow climbing frame for, 152–153
  miniature gardens in, 76–79
  plant ideas for, 119
  tropical plants in, how to prepare, 178–179
Country cabin retreat, on flower farm, 132–137
Country style, shed decorated in, 62

Craft studio, repurposed shed as, 54

D

Davis, Laura, compact urban garden of, 90–95
Decorative glass, 28–29
Dining alfresco. *See* Alfresco dining spaces
DIY projects
  how-to instructions, 140–181
  simple decorative displays, 182–185
Dragonfly decorations, how to make, 146–147
Dubé, Chrystiane, garden of, 106–114

E

Eclectic backyard retreat, 19
Enamelware, uses for, 105
English-style backyard retreat, 15

F

Fernandez, Patty, garden of, 82–89
Firepits, 130
  barbecue, how to make, 160–161
  propane, in contemporary garden setting, 74
Fish decorations, how to make, 148–149
Flags and bunting, how to make, 170–171
Fliniau, Holly, garden of, 116–121
Floating candles, 74, 182
Floral swag, as table runner, 68
Flower borders, 102
Flower bouquets, hand-tied, how to prepare, 176–177
Flower farm, country cabin retreat on, 132–137
Flower-pot man sculpture, 109
Folk art statue, 108
Folly, repurposed shed as, 58
Footbridge, homemade, 112–113
Fountain, wall, 88
Front gardens, 96–105, 118
Funnels, as string holders, 183

G

Galvanized buckets/containers, as planters, 99, 127
Garden Candy tomato seeds, how to grow, 180–181
Garden gates, 85, 109
Garden rooms, decking creating, 106–107
Garden sheds, repurposed as retreats, 54–63
  with colorful fabrics, 63
  country style, 62
  cozy, 60
  craft studio, 55
  folly, with living roof, 58
  homestyle retreat, 60
  modern abode, 59
  outdoor office, 56
  plant-filled glassless greenhouse, 57
  in rustic style, 63
  sewing room, 61
  in shabby-chic style, 63
  tearoom, 54
  with warm wood flooring, 63
Garden stakes, handmade, 104–105
Garden (summer) house, in urban oasis, 93–95
Gardens
  creatively inspired examples, 82–137
  in front of house, 96–105, 118
  miniature, 76–79
  as retreats. *See* Backyard retreats
Glass, decorative, 28–29
Glassless greenhouse, plant-filled, 57
Gourd bird feeder, how to make, 142–143
Greenhouse, glassless, 57

H

Hand-tied flower bouquets, how to prepare, 176–177
Hanging planters
  chandelier, 32
  colander, 184
  hazel branch frame for, 49
  two-handled teacup, 35
Hazel branch frame, for hanging baskets, 49
Henricks, Karen, front garden of, 96–105
Herbs, planters for
  colander, 184
  medicinal herb garden, how to make, 154–155
  tin cans in vertical grid pattern, 51
Heron sculpture, 111
Homestyle retreat, repurposed shed as, 60
Household objects, as planters, 30–33
Hutch, for potted plant display, 185

I

Industrial-styled backyard retreat, 20–21
Iron daybed, beneath shed lean-to, 89

J

Jungle-styled backyard retreat, 23

L

Lace, vintage, 86–87
Ladders, 102, 115
  for ornament display, 183
  for potted plant displays, 24–25, 50
Ladybug decorations, how to make, 150–151
Lanterns
  paper, 74, 164
  tin can, how to make, 168–169
Light bulb vases, how to make, 140–141

Lighting. *See* Candles/Candleholders; Outdoor lighting; String lights; Tea lights
Living roof
 on birdhouse, how to make, 166–167
 on garden shed, 58
Living walls/displays, 52–53, 124

M
Maple seeds, making dragonfly decorations from, 146–147
Me time. *See* Backyard retreats; Garden sheds, repurposed as retreats
Medicinal herb garden, how to make, 154–155
Metal pieces
 containers, 127
 rusted. *See* Rusted metal pieces
 suspended cans, as wall planters, 53
Meyer lemons, dwarf, 96, 102
Miniature gardens, 76–79
Mirrors, use in garden, 26–27, 32, 116, 122, 130
Modern arbor, with seating pod, 125, 126
Modern backyard retreat, 14
Mosaic
 in African-styled backyard retreat, 10–11
 on terra-cotta pots/saucers, how to add, 144–145, 184
 water feature with, 26

N
Natural remedies, medicinal herb garden for, 154–155
Nesting boxes. *See* Birdhouses

O
Office, repurposed shed as, 56, 94–95
Outdoor curtains, 88
Outdoor lighting, 70–75, 92
 antique streetlights, 112–113
 with paper pompoms, ideas for, 164–165
 solar-powered, 99
 tiki-style torches, 72, 184
 tin can lanterns, how to make, 168–169
 uplighting, 75
Outdoor office, repurposed shed as, 56, 94–95
Outdoor rooms
 decking creating, 106–107
 screens creating. *See* Privacy screens
Outdoor shower, 134–135
Outdoor storage
 display as, 127
 wooden bookcase as, 162–163
 wooden crates as, 31, 174–175

P
Pallet planters, 49
 how to make, 156–157
Paper pompoms, how to make, 164–165
Pavers
 brick, 80–81, 110, 115, 119
 stone. *See* Stone pavers
Picture box potted plant display, 131
Planters, ideas for, 30–33
 birdhouses as, 47
 galvanized buckets as, 99, 127
 hanging. *See* Hanging planters
 metal wash tub, 105
 from pallets. *See* Pallet planters
 pocket planters, for vertical display, 53
 wagon wheel, how to make, 158–159
 wheelbarrow as. *See* Wheelbarrow, as planter
Plantings
 for backyard retreat styles, 10–19
 in creatively inspired gardens, 82–137
 for medicinal herb garden, 154–155
 for miniature gardens, 76–79
Pocket planters, for vertical display, 53
Pompoms, making from tissue paper, 164–165
Pond, with outdoor room, 106–107
Pots. *See* Terra-cotta pots/saucers
Potted plant displays
 hutch for, 185
 ladders for, 24–25, 50
 pallets for. *See* Pallet planters
 picture box for, 131
 timber shelving for, 50, 127, 131
 weathered boards for, 48
Potting benches, 38–41, 121
Pressed-flower candles, 72
Privacy screens
 living walls as, 52, 124
 materials and uses for, 123, 124–125

Q
Quilts, as table coverings, 64, 86–87

R
Ratté, Roland, garden of, 106–114
Retreats
 garden. *See* Backyard retreats
 sheds as. *See* Garden sheds, repurposed as retreats
Romantic vintage-styled backyard retreat, 12–13
Rotary phone, as planter, 183
Rusted metal pieces
 containers for succulents, 125, 126
 for industrial-styled backyard retreat, 21–21
 on timber screen, 131
 use in living wall, 52
Rustic style, shed decorated in, 63

S
Screens. *See* Privacy screens

Sculptures
bucket lady, how to construct, 172–173
flower-pot man, 109
heron, 111
Seaside-styled backyard retreat, 16–17
Seasonal table decor, 68–69, 164
Sewing room, repurposed shed as, 61
Shabby-chic decor
country cabin retreat, 132–137
repurposed shed decorated in, 63
She sheds. *See* Garden sheds, repurposed as retreats
Shed lean-to, iron daybed beneath, 89
Sheds. *See* Garden sheds, repurposed as retreats
Shipping container, repurposed as outdoor dining space, 59
Slide, between garden levels, 129
Small gardens, 82–89, 96–105. *See also* Front gardens
compact urban, 90–95
miniature, 76–79
Solar-powered lights, 99
Stone pavers
dragonfly, 102
plants between, 86–88
Stones
large freestanding, 112–114
small flat, making bee and ladybug decorations from, 150–151
String lights, 71, 73
Succulents
for birdhouse living roof, 166–167
in multitiered garden, 122–131
in teacups, 34–35
in wooden crate planter, 30
Suitcase
miniature garden in, 76
as special-occasion gift holder, 184
Sunroom, open air, 120
Sycamore seeds, making dragonfly decorations from, 146–147

T

Table decor, for alfresco dining, 64, 68–69, 84, 86–87, 104, 136–137, 164
Tea lights, 11, 12, 72–73, 165
floating, 182
in tiki-style torches, 184
Teacups/Teapots
as birdhouses, 46
as planters, 32, 34–37
Tearoom, repurposed shed as, 54
Terra-cotta pots/saucers
display on/under potting bench, 121
mosaic-clad, how to make, 144–145, 184
painted flower-pot man sculpture, 109
Tiki-style torches
rattan, 72
with terra-cotta pots, 184
Timber, recycled shelving, 50
Timber, weathered
for gate and fencing, 85
outdoor storage display, 127
for vertical display, 48
Tin cans
artwork created from, 183
as decorative lanterns, how to make, 168–169
as planters, 32, 49, 51
Traditional backyard retreat, 15
Trellis, painted, as focal point, 49
Trompe l'oeil effects, 27
Tropical plants
in container gardens, how to prepare, 178–179
for jungle-styled backyard retreat, 23

U

Uplighting, 75
Urban backyard, compact, 90–95

V

Vases, light bulb, how to make, 140–141
Vertical plant displays, 52–53, 124
Votives, 69, 73. *See also* Tea lights

W

Wagon wheels
hanging planters from, 31
as planter, how to make, 158–159
Wall fountain, 88
Warm wood flooring, repurposed shed with, 63
Wash tub, as planter, 105
Water features
in African-styled backyard retreat, 10–11
amid birdhouse display, 114
with floating candles, 74, 182
in industrial-styled backyard retreat, 20
mosaic, 26
wall fountain, 88
Wells, Steven, multitiered backyard of, 122–131
Wheelbarrow, as planter, 100–101
for miniature garden, 79
Whimsical backyard retreat, 18
Whimsical bucket lady decoration, how to make, 172–173
Wildflowers, in urban oasis, 91
Willow branches
crafting plant climbing frame from, 152–153
making fish decorations from, 148–149
Wisteria canopy, 66
Wooden crates
for outdoor hanging storage, 31
for outdoor storage, how to make, 174–175
as planters, 30
Wooden pallets. *See* Pallet planters

COVER Mark Lohman **2-3** Maria Kovalevskaya / EyeEm/Getty Images **4-5** GAP Photos; GAP Interiors/David Giles; GAP Photos/Victoria Firmston; GAP Photos/Brent Wilson; wwing/Getty Images; facfotodigital/Getty Images(2) **6-7** Solomiia Kratsylo/Getty Images **8-9** Oreolife / Alamy Stock Photo **10-11** GAP Photos/Clive Nichols; GAP Photos/Howard Rice; Mark Scott/Gap Interiors; GAP Photos/Howard Rice **12-13** GAP Photos/ Hanneke Reijbroek; GAP Photos/Lynn Keddie; GAP Photos/Pernilla Bergdahl; GAP Photos/Elke Borkowski **14-15** GAP Photos/Brent Wilson; GAP Photos/Brent Wilson **16-17** GAP Photos/Marcus Harpur–Owner: Geoff Stonebanks, Driftwood garden, Seaford, East Sussex; GAP Photos/Nicola Stocken; GAP Photos/Julia Boulton; GAP Photos/Clive Nichols–Design: Mark Laurence **18-19** GAP Photos/Robert Mabic; GAP Interiors/ Ingrid Rasmussen; GAP Photos/Jason Ingram–Design: Grenville Johnson and Alan Elms; GAP Photos/ The CONTENTed Nest; GAP Photos/Heather Edwards **20-21** GAP Photos/Dianna Jazwinski–Design: Adrian Hallam, Chris Arrowsmith and Nigel Dunnett; GAP Photos(2); GAP Photos/Richard Bloom–Designed by Darren Hawkes, Sponsored by Coutts **22-23** GAP Photos/Brent Wilson; GAP Interiors/Ingrid Rasmussen; GAP Photos/Jason Ingram–Design: Grenville Johnson and Alan Elms; GAP; Photos/Heather Edwards; GAP Photos/The CONTENTed Nest **24-25** GAP Photos/Jerry Pavia; GAP Photos/Maxine Adcock; GAP Photos/Elke Borkowski; GAP Photos/Friedrich Strauss; GAP Photos/Manuela Goehner **26-27** GAP Photos/Nicola Stocken; GAP Photos; GAP Photos/Graham Strong; GAP Interiors/Caroline Mardon–Stylist: Alexandra Toso; GAP Photos/ John Glover–design: Anne Frith **28-29** GAP Interiors/House and Leisure - Stylist: Heather Boting; GAP Photos/ Carole Drake; GAP Photos/Richard Bloom–Designed by Jim Bishop **30-31** GAP Photos/Dianna Jazwinski; GAP Photos/Juliette Wade; GAP Photos; GAP Photos/www.futurecontenthub.com **32-33** GAP Interiors/Maxwell Attenborough; GAP Interiors/David Giles; GAP Photos; Gap Photos; GAP Photos/Victoria Firmston **34-35** GAP Photos/Julia Boulton; GAP Photos/Friedrich Strauss **36-37** GAP Photos; GAP Photos/Juliette Wade; GAP Photos/ Julia Boulton; GAP Photos/Victoria Firmston **38-39** www.futurecontenthub.com; GAP Photos/Elke Borkowski; GAP Interiors/Mark Scott; GAP Photos/Elke Borkowski; www.futurecontenthub.com **40-41** GAP Photos; GAP Photos/Friedrich Strauss; www.futurecontenthub.com; GAP Photos/Friedrich Strauss; GAP Photos/Anna Omiotek-Tott–Designer: Ruth Gwynn & Alan Williams **42-43** GAP Photos/Heather Edwards; GAP Photos/FhF Greenmedia **44-45** GAP Photos/Carole Drake - Kincora, Somerset; GAP Photos/Elke Borkowski **46-47** GAP Photos/Visions; GAP Photos/Perry Mastrovito; GAP Photos/Visions; GAP Photos/Perry Mastrovito; GAP Photos/ Jerry Pavia **48-49** GAP Photos/Brent Wilson; GAP Photos(2); GAP Photos//Juliette Wade; GAP Photos; www.futurecontenthub.com **50-51** GAP Photos/Fiona Lea; GAP Photos/Brent Wilson; GAP Photos; GAP Photos/ Friedrich Strauss; GAP Photos **52-53** GAP Photos/Richard Bloom–Future Nature, designed by Adrian Hallam, Chris Arrowsmith and Nigel Dunnett sponsored by Yorkshire; GAP Photos; GAP Photos/Rob Whitworth–Four Corners garden–Design Peter Reader, RHS Hampton Court Flower Show; GAP Photos; GAP Photos/Lynn Keddie **54-55** www.futurecontenthub.com (2) **56-57** www.futurecontenthub.com(2) **58-59** GAP Photos/Elke Borkowski–Design: Tony Wagstaff; GAP Photos/Andrea Jones–Design: Ann-Marie Powell **60-61** GAP Interiors/ David Giles; GAP Interiors/Nadia Mackenzie **62-63** GAP Interiors/Nick Carter(2); GAP Interiors/Clive Nichols–Design: Kaffe Fassett; GAP Interiors/Richard Gadsby; GAP Interiors/Douglas Gibb **64-65** GAP Interiors/Robin Stubbert; GAP Interiors/Nikki Crisp **66-67** GAP Photos/Nicola Stocken; GAP Interiors/Mark Scott; Lizzie Orme/ Future Publishing LTD; GAP Interiors/House and Leisure–Styling Mia Vincent–Photographs Micky Hoyle; GAP Photos/Friedrich Strauss **68-69** GAP Interiors/Mark Scott; GAP Photos/Friedrich Strauss; GAP Photos; GAP Photos/Victoria Firmston; GAP Photos/Friedrich Strauss; GAP Photos/Friedrich Strauss **70-71** GAP Photos/ Nicola Stocken; GAP Interiors/Mark Scott **72-73** GAP Photos/Friedrich Strauss; GAP Photos/Victoria Firmston; GAP Photos/Friedrich Strauss; www.futurecontenthub.com **74-75** GAP Photos/Friedrich Strauss; GAP Photos–Design: Cube 1994; GAP Photos/Victoria Firmston; GAP Photos/Elke Borkowski–Design: Fritz Doepper; GAP Photos/Victoria Firmston; GAP Photos/Friedrich Strauss **76-77** GAP Photos; GAP Photos/Nicola Stocken **78-79** GAP Photos; GAP Photos/Jerry Pavia **80-81** Solomiia Kratsylo/GettyImages **82-83** Mark Lohman **84-85** Mark Lohman(2) **86-87** Mark Lohman **88-89** Mark Lohman(4) **90-91** Time Inc (UK) Ltd **92-93** Time Inc

(UK) Ltd(4) **94–95** Time Inc (UK) Ltd(2) **96–97** Mark Lohman **98–99** Mark Lohman(4) **100–101** Mark Lohman **102–103** Mark Lohman(4) **104–105** Mark Lohman(4) **106–107** GAP Photos/Perry Mastrovito **108–109** GAP Photos/Perry Mastrovito(4) **110–111** GAP Photos/Perry Mastrovito(2) **112–113** GAP Photos/Perry Mastrovito **114–115** GAP Photos/Perry Mastrovito(2) **116–117** Mark Lohman **118–119** Mark Lohman(4) **120–121** Mark Lohman(2) **122–123**GAP Photos/Brent Wilson(2) **124–125** GAP Photos/Brent Wilson(4) **126–127** GAP Photos/ Brent Wilson(5) **128–129** GAP Photos/Brent Wilson(2) **130–131** GAP Photos/Brent Wilson(5) **132–133** GAP Interiors/Robin Stubbert(2) **134–135** GAP Interiors/Robin Stubbert(4) **136–137** GAP Interiors/Robin Stubbert(5) **138–139** Petri Oeschger/Getty Images **140–141** GAP Photos/Victoria Firmston(5) **142–143** GAP Photos(7) **144–145** GAP Photos(7) **146–147** GAP Photos/Victoria Firmston(5) **148–149** GAP Photos(7) **150–151** GAP Photos/ Victoria Firmston(4) **152–153** GAP Photos(7) **154–155** GAP Photos(7) **156–157** GAP Photos(7) **158–159** GAP Photos/ Nicola Stocken(7) **160–161** GAP Photos(5) **162–163** GAP Photos(7) **164–165** GAP Photos/Victoria Firmston(7) **166–167** GAP Photos(7) **168–169** GAP Photos(4) **170–171** GAP Photos/Maxine Adcock(5) **172–173** GAP Photos(5) **174–175** GAP Photos(5) **176–177** GAP Photos(5) **178–179** GAP Photos(5) **180–181** GAP Photos(7) **182–183** GAP Photos; GAP Interiors/Colin Poole; GAP Interiors/Dan Duchars; GAP Photos/Howard Rice; GAP Photos/Marcus Harpur **184–185** GAP Photos/Victoria Firmston; GAP Photos/Friedrich Strauss; GAP Photos(2); GAP Photos/ Gary Smith **BACK COVER** Rosemary Calvert/Getty Imges; Maria Cristina Gonzalez / EyeEm/Getty Images; Rosemary Calvert/Getty images; Claudia Rehm, Red Chopsticks Images/Getty Images; Mark Lohman; GAP Photos/Jerry Pavia

An Imprint of
Centennial Media, LLC
1111 Brickell Avenue, 10th Floor
Miami, FL 33131, U.S.A.

ISBN 978-1-951274-98-6

Distributed by
Simon & Schuster, Inc.
1230 Avenue of the Americas
New York, NY 10020, U.S.A.

For information about custom editions, special sales and premium and corporate purchases, please contact Centennial Media at contact@centennialmedia.com.

Manufactured in China

10 9 8 7 6 5 4 3 2 1